THE TEACHER-CURRICULUM ENCOUNTER

SUNY Series in Curriculum Issues and Inquiries
Edmund C. Short, EDITOR

THE TEACHER-CURRICULUM ENCOUNTER

Freeing Teachers from the Tyranny of Texts

Miriam Ben-Peretz

with foreword by
Lee S. Shulman

State University of New York Press

Published by
State University of New York Press, Albany

Printed in the United States of America
by Princeton University Press

For information,
address the State University of New York Press,
State University Plaza, Albany, NY 12246

Library of Congress Cataloguing-in-Publication Data
Ben-Peretz, Miriam.
  The teacher-curriculum encounter : freeing teachers
from the tyranny of texts / by Miriam Ben-Peretz : with
foreword by Lee Shulman.
      p. cm.—(SUNY series in curriculum issues and
inquiries)
  Includes bibliographical references.
  ISBN 0-7914-0375-0.—ISBN 0-7914-0376-9 (pbk.)
  1. Curriculum planning. 2. Teachers—Training of.
I. Title. II. Series.
LB2806.15.B46 1990   89-28867
375'.001—dc20   CIP

10   9   8   7   6   5   4   3   2   1

Contents

Foreword

Lee S. Shulman, Stanford University

Curriculum and teaching have long been treated as opposites, akin to hot and cold, war and peace, or sadness and joy. Curriculum dealt with the carefully planned organization of the subject matter in the form of written materials, units of instruction and other stable products of deliberation, design, writing and editing. Teaching, on the other hand, was interactive, swift, episodic and spontaneous. Though often planned, it was typically adaptive and reactive. While curriculum might be the backdrop for teaching, the two were not to be confused.

True, there were theorists who recognized that the manifest curriculum was not always as it appeared. Some pointed out that curriculum could be hidden, exerting its impact on students insidiously. Others explained that curriculum was not that which was proposed, but what was taught; only once actually implemented could we know the effective curriculum. Thus, the real curriculum is that experienced in classrooms, not the published texts and teachers' manuals.

Miriam Ben-Peretz has introduced a strikingly new and important perspective into these discussions, especially for those of us concerned with the preparation and professional development of teachers. About fifteen years ago she began to write of "curriculum potential," a view that attacks the opposition of curriculum and teaching and points up the ways in which the two ideas are mutually supportive and reinforcing.

Ben-Peretz argues that curriculum must be understood as both far too much and far too little, as providing more than any teacher could possibly use, and yet less than any teacher really requires. The essential value of curriculum is how it permits teachers to adapt, invent and transform as they confront the realities of classroom life. Teaching is neither opposed to curriculum, nor does teaching alone define curriculum. Indeed, even curriculum that is designed by teachers (another topic with which Ben-Peretz is concerned in this volume) must be understood in terms of its potential for teaching.

The theoretical work of this book is squarely in the traditions of the late Joseph Schwab. His writings about practical deliberation in curriculum development emphasized the complexities of curriculum, the need for deliberations about curriculum to be eclectic in disciplinary terms and pluralistic in the multiple perspectives that must be brought to bear on its creation. Schwab said little, however, about the preparation of teachers to work with a curriculum so conceived, much less the preparation of such teachers. Here the work of Ben-Peretz builds on that of Schwab, extending and enriching that earlier thinking.

The orientation of this book makes it particularly germane to those concerned with the reform of teacher education and the growing movements toward teacher professionalization. Teachers must be prepared to serve as acute critics, analysts and adaptors of curriculum. They must learn to understand curriculum as providing the raw material from which they can craft and shape the instruction of their pupils. In principle, no curriculum is adequate because it cannot anticipate the infinite variations of students, teachers and contexts. Yet teachers cannot be expected to produce curriculum by themselves as they encounter these situations. Thus, a partnership is needed, in which teachers draw from the potential of curriculum and transform its ideas and materials into activities and representations that connect with learners appropriately. The challenge to teacher educators is profound. Preparing teachers who can work individually and collectively in this way is no mean achievement.

The conception of a teaching profession implicit in this work is also timely. There is no room for the image of a passive teacher obligated to implement the curriculum, be it locally or nationally mandated. The teacher's professional mandate is to treat the curriculum with respect and care. It represents the best work of other educators who have drawn from their own knowledge of subject matter and of children to present for the teacher's consideration a body of materials and ideas of vast potential. Now the teacher's work begins, as this potential is realized only through the most intelligent and considered pedagogical work by a well-trained and seriously committed professional.

I have learned a great deal from Miriam Ben-Peretz during the past fifteen years. We have become colleagues-at-a-distance and good friends as well as scholars who work adjoining fields. It is a privilege and pleasure to write this foreword to a book I am confident will inform the work of a generation of curriculum developers, teachers and teacher educators.

Acknowledgments

This book has grown over years of involvement in curriculum development with teachers. I am most grateful to the teachers with whom I have been fortunate to work in development teams, in schools, and in graduate courses, for the insights they provided on the teacher-curriculum encounter.

Several scholars have given me encouragement and guidance. I am particularly grateful to Professor Edmund C. Short, editor of this series for his support and help.

I owe much to Professor Michael F. Connelly, the Ontario Institute for Studies in Education, with whom I shared many hours of discussion on curricular themes, and I am pleased for this opportunity to thank him. For their constructive and perceptive comments I thank Professor Sharon Feiman-Nemser, Michigan State University; Professor Jean D. Clandinin, Calgary University; Dr. Moshe Silberstein, Tel-Aviv University, and Margot Lifmann, University of Haifa.

I am deeply indebted to Professor Seymour Fox, the Hebrew University, Jerusalem, who has introduced me to curriculum studies. I wish to express my profound and sincere gratefulness to Professor Lee S. Shulman, Stanford University, for his insightful and encouraging remarks, for suggesting this book's title, and for writing the foreword.

Special thanks are due to Lois G. Patton, Editor-in-Chief, and to Christine M. Lynch, Production Editor, of the State University of New York Press, for their constructive advice and comments.

For their dedicated assistance in the difficult task of editing, typing and proofreading, I express my gratitude and appreciation to Anat Zajdman, Sabina Szaikowski and Miriam Dembo.

Finally, I wish to express my deep gratitude to my husband, Moshe Ben-Peretz, for his constant support through all stages of this work.

Introduction

"Oh, to be a teacher
Now that planning's in the air"
Jane Hope, Scholarship at Stake, *1953, p. 102*

One of the main features of teaching is its reliance on textbooks and other kinds of curriculum materials, such as teachers' guidelines. Teachers fulfill many functions in their classrooms, from monitoring their students' behavior to lecturing, administering, questioning, assessing, and correcting. These and other teaching activities are carried out in the context of using some form of curriculum. There is evidence that teachers tend to cherish their curricular autonomy, for instance, the right to choose teaching materials. Jackson (1968) cites teachers who protest strongly against the possibility of restricting this right. On the other hand, research shows that many teachers teach the textbook and are not involved in decisions about ways of presenting the materials (Goodlad 1984; Jackson 1986). In such situations adaptations of curriculum materials to the needs of diverse student populations may be extremely limited.

Teachers tend to rely on a variety of curriculum materials, such as textbooks or workbooks, as sources for their lesson planning. How are these materials related to the school curriculum? Connelly and Clandinin (1988) suggest the idea that "curriculum is something experienced in situations" (p. 6). They maintain that these experiences take place "through processes of interaction with things, things we call 'curriculum materials.' For a person, growth into the future through experience in the curriculum is, therefore, a process of interacting with curriculum materials" (p. 137). Classroom interactions of teachers and students with curriculum materials involve instructional processes which are devised and organized by teachers and which are enacted in changing classroom situations. Curriculum materials are the "texts" used by teachers in their daily professional lives. These "texts" may be read and interpreted in different ways. The central idea of this book is that curriculum materials, the "texts," are more than the embodiment of their developers' intentions, and offer teachers a wide array of *curriculum potential* depending on their purposes and the demands of their classroom situations. Teachers need knowledge and expertise in uncovering the potential of curriculum materials so that these can be reconstructed for particular students and for specific classroom situations.

This book is for teachers in that it addresses needs for the professional and efficient use of curriculum materials and for more creative and reflective teacher involvement in the curriculum process. This book is also for school curriculum consultants, department heads, and curriculum developers who are concerned about the meagre results of manifold costly attempts to improve education through the production of curriculum materials. Practitioners who are involved in curricular issues may find the notions of 'curriculum potential' and 'curriculum interpretation' useful for creating and working with curriculum materials.

Last, but not least, this book is for scholars and students in the curriculum domain. It focuses on curriculum decision making by teachers, pulling together some of the existing literature. It deals with the complex relationship among teachers, their students, and the curriculum materials they use. It permits a glimpse into the teacher-curriculum encounter and some of its key issues.

The main theme of the book revolves around the following notions:

1. Teachers fulfill a variety of functions regarding the creation and implementation of curriculum materials, their curriculum "texts."
2. Teachers may be autonomous in their decisions about the appropriate use of curriculum materials.
3. Curriculum materials are far richer in their potential than is envisaged by their developers, and offer teachers a wide array of possible uses.
4. The interpretation of curriculum materials, which reveals their potential for classroom use, is a vital stage in teachers' lesson planning.
5. The interpretation of curriculum materials allows teachers to express their individual approaches to teaching, as well as their responses to the needs of their specific classroom situation. The creative "reading" of curricu-

lum materials, as well as their flexible use in classrooms, is conceived as "freeing teachers from the tyranny of the text."

6. The interpretation of curriculum materials is a complex
   process which requires curriculum literacy. Interpretation may be guided by different frameworks and be carried out with the aid of various instruments.

7. The realization of curriculum potential may serve to reduce the need for continuous external curriculum development because of teachers' greater involvement in
   the transformation and reconstruction of existing materials to fit their individual approaches and the dynam-
   ics of their specific educational situations.

8. Defensible and flexible uses of curriculum materials by
   informed teachers may diminish some of their concerns
   relating to curriculum.

To sum it up: teachers are encouraged to see their major role in the
partnership of curriculum development as that of informed and
creative interpreters who are prepared to reflect on their curriculum and to reconstruct it.

The first chapter presents readers with a glimpse into two
cases of teachers' involvement in different curricular functions.
The first is a case of curriculum implementation, and the second is
a case of curriculum development by teachers. The "tale" of two
curricular cases leads to some conclusions about the active role
teachers could play whenever they create or use any form of curriculum materials.

Chapter 2 starts with definitions of *curriculum* and goes on to
a more detailed description of curricular forms that teachers may
encounter. Several distinctions which are considered relevant for
teachers are discussed: mandated versus open (self-initiated) curricula; structured, sequential, versus unstructured, modular curriculum materials; detailed versus general curriculum; and long-
term versus short-term curricular planning. Everyday curricular
activities of teachers are exemplified.

Chapter 3 addresses some of the concerns teachers have regarding curricular issues. The chapter starts with the question,
What do teachers want to know about curriculum materials? Some
research findings are presented which highlight teachers' concerns
with the "subject matter" and "student" aspects of the curricu-

lum. The major teacher concerns mentioned in this chapter are as
follows:

1. The issue of *coverage*, breadth versus depth in teaching
   any subject matter—how do I choose?
2. Expectations regarding adherence to the curriculum—
   how do I adapt and change existing curriculum materials to my own teaching situation?
3. Creating my own curriculum—do I have the necessary
   curriculum knowledge?

Reports on the conclusions of an analysis of several curriculum
guides lead to a brief discussion of the functions and roles assigned to teachers by curriculum developers.

The central question addressed in Chapter 4 concerns the nature of curriculum materials and their possible adaptation to diverse needs and circumstances. The definition and elaboration of
the concept 'curriculum potential' are at the core of this chapter.
It is argued that curriculum materials lend themselves to a variety
of interpretations beyond the intentions of their developers, offering manifold opportunities for diverse uses in the classroom. The
distinctions between *curriculum potential, unintended outcomes*, the
hidden curriculum, and the *null curriculum* are discussed. Various
examples of uncovering curriculum potential in different subject
matter areas are presented. Some basic differences between the
uncovering of curriculum potential by developers of materials, and
by teachers who use these materials, are discussed. The need for
special interpretative abilities is emphasized.

Chapter 5 describes and explains various modes of curriculum
interpretation. Distinctions are made between *subjective* and *objective* modes of interpretation, and between *internal* and *external*
schemes of analysis which may lead to curriculum interpretation.
Internal schemes of analysis rely on characteristics of curriculum
materials which were explicitly stated by their developers. External schemes of analysis apply external categories derived from educational frameworks to the process of curriculum interpretation.
Examples of the uses of a variety of analytic schemes are provided.
The chapter ends with an example of one teacher's reading of the
curriculum potential of one curricular item.

Chapter 6 presents four instruments and procedures designed
to aid teachers in the process of curriculum interpretation that
leads to the uncovering of curriculum potential. These instruments

exemplify some of the distinctions made in Chapter 5, namely, the distinction between subjective and objective interpretation and the distinction between internal and external frames of reference for curriculum analysis and interpretation. The use of these instruments and procedures is exemplified in different subject matter areas.

The last chapter confronts the issue of using teacher education for revealing and employing curriculum potential. Possible implications of the notions of curriculum potential and curriculum interpretation for pre- and in-service teacher education programs are discussed. Several strategies of teacher education are proposed. This issue is connected to notions of teacher autonomy and teacher empowerment. The relationships between teacher concerns regarding curriculum matters and the development of curriculum literacy are discussed.

1

Patterns of Teachers' Involvement in the Curriculum Endeavor

"No action is without side effects"
Commoners's law of ecology
Paul Dickson, The Official Rules, *1978, p. 30*

Curriculum topics and materials are prominent elements of the culture of schools. The choice of content for teaching, the nature of instructional materials, and the preferred modes of using these determine, to a large extent, the environment in which teachers, students, and materials interact in the teaching-learning process. Curriculum materials are the tools of the trade of teaching. The adoption of appropriate materials and their skillful adaptation to specific classroom situations will either facilitate or hinder the teaching efforts of even the most dedicated of teachers.

The dominating form of curricula at all school levels is textbooks (Goodlad 1984). Reviewing teachers' school practices, Fullan claims that "teachers frequently take and teach the textbook" (Fullan 1982, p. 118). It seems that textbooks play a central role in the planning of lessons by teachers, who decide in what order to treat the various chapters of the textbook and how much time to devote to each one. The choice and use of textbooks, or other kinds of curriculum materials, seem to constitute the major curricular function of teachers. Teachers' function as implementors of curricular materials, which are developed by agents outside their classrooms, raises the issue of adherence to the given text versus teacher autonomy to introduce changes and modifications. This issue is the central theme examined in this book.

Use of external curriculum materials in the form of textbooks is not the only mode of teacher involvement in the curriculum endeavor. Teachers may also be engaged in centralized, or in school-based, curriculum development. We shall examine possible links

1

between these two curricular functions of teachers, as curriculum implementors and as curriculum creators.

Two case studies form the basis for describing and analyzing the major ways in which teachers may become involved in curriculum efforts. One case study deals with teachers' use of externally developed curriculum materials. The second case study focuses on teachers' involvement in a curriculum development project in which they created their own curriculum materials.[1]

TEACHERS' USE OF EXTERNALLY DEVELOPED CURRICULUM MATERIALS

We start with an analysis of a case of curriculum implementation. It deals with teachers' use of externally developed curriculum materials, their interpretation of the materials, and the manner in which they adapted them for their classrooms (Ben-Peretz and Silberstein 1982).

The case study was an investigation of the metamorphosis which occurs in the process of transforming scholarly knowledge into curricular materials in classroom use. At the first level of transformation, curriculum developers decided on the following issues: What ideas, principles, and concepts were suitable for inclusion in the curriculum material? What information should be covered and what omitted? What aspects should be emphasized? What meaningful aspects for students and society could be dealt with by means of the chosen content? What opportunities for cognitive and affective development of students could be incorporated into the curricular material?

At the second level of transformation, teachers who used the curriculum materials, the guidelines, textbooks, and audiovisual aids devised learning experiences which were based on their interpretation of the materials. In this process teachers may modify the materials or may adhere to the text, may try to cover the prescribed curriculum or may decide to use only parts of it. The case presented herewith may serve as a concrete example of teachers' decisions in their use of curriculum materials.

The curriculum unit in this case was a topic in a biology course which had already been taught for several years in junior high schools. This unit is part of a student textbook in botany intended for the eighth grade: The Plant and its Environment (1974). The textbook itself is one component of a junior high school curriculum package in biology which includes student textbooks, teacher guides and instructional aids such as films. It is related to the following issue: Is it possible to reduce the amount of water used in irrigation of citrus trees? and was designated for two lesson periods. The unit described several experiments related to the water consumption of plants, and raised issues of basic research and its potential contribution to socioeconomic problems. The unit had been prepared by a group of curriculum experts, teachers, and subject matter specialists acting as a team at a national Centre for Curriculum Development.

For the purpose of analyzing the implementation process, twenty teachers were randomly chosen from a list of teachers who had taught the unit. They were approached and asked to respond in writing to several questions relating to the following issues:

- The actual time they had devoted to teaching the unit
- The extent of their adherence to the recommendations in the teachers' guide
- The elements of content chosen and emphasized by the teachers
- A description of instructional strategies used in teaching the unit
- An indication of the context in which the unit had been taught, its place in the sequence of teaching, and its linkage to other topics

Teachers were asked to provide reasons and considerations leading to their actions in using this unit. The teachers were also asked to provide a short description of their student population and some background data about the school. These background data were necessary to an understanding of the context of teaching and the teachers' decisions in relation to their concrete classroom situations. The reports prepared by the teachers are interpreted as expressing their perception of the teaching-learning situations as planned and created by them. Teachers' perceptions of the mode of curriculum implementation they adopted are considered in relation to their "autonomy space" as decision makers. The analysis of teachers' responses provided some glimpses into the kinds of transformations which take place in the process of implementing external curricular materials.

Findings from this Case of Curriculum Implementation

According to Fullan (1982), "the time perspective is one of the most neglected aspects of the implementation process" (p. 68). Yet teachers make daily decisions about time allocations and timing of instruction. In our case the teachers' guide recommended, for instance, that two periods be devoted to teaching the unit. Ten of the responding teachers stated that they did indeed allocate between one and two periods to this unit. However, the other teachers needed three, four, or more periods for teaching the same unit. Since the unit was one of the first in the set of curriculum materials, this may be why some teachers devoted extra time to it. At the beginning of the course teachers may not feel under any pressure of time. They may also be concerned with covering all the materials, which will lead to an extension of the recommended instructional time.

Twelve of the twenty teachers replied that they adhered to the teachers' handbook in their teaching. How did this faithfulness express itself in the ways in which teachers used the materials? What aspects of content did they emphasize? What educational themes, topics, and principles of knowledge did they try to transmit to their students? We may view these themes, topics, and principles as the educational messages embodied in the text. Teachers' choice of "educational messages" determines to a large extent the scope of possible learning outcomes and achievements. Some of these "educational messages" are stated explicitly in the curriculum text, for instance, in a passage related to the importance of learning about scientific research methods. Yet implicit messages, the hidden curriculum, accompany the teaching process.

In this specific case the teachers' guide lists four "educational messages" to be emphasized in teaching the unit. An analysis of the information received from teachers about their choice of themes and principles indicated the following selection patterns (shown as percentages of total references to all themes emphasized by the teachers):

1. Gaining insights into issues involved in conflict situations between the needs of individuals (e.g. free water consumption) and the public good (water conservation for agricultural purposes)—29 percent
2. Understanding the research design described in the unit and its various components—23 percent
3. Understanding the relationship between the interpretation of data collected in an experiment and the drawing of conclusions—23 percent

4. Perceiving possible links between research and societal needs—18 percent

In addition to these four themes, which were indicated in the teachers' guide, another 7 percent of the "educational messages" reported by the teachers concerned issues not explicitly listed in the guide, such as "learning about agriculture."

It is interesting to note that, in contrast to the degree of freedom which they permitted themselves in allocating time to the teaching of this unit, teachers generally adhered to the teachers' guide with regard to the educational themes, the "messages," which they handled in the course of their instruction. Only 7 percent of the issues and principles emphasized by the teachers went beyond the suggestions in their teachers' guide. It should be added that, although the teachers did not, in fact, reveal a significant variety of possible different themes in the curriculum materials, they did express their professional autonomy in deciding on the relative importance which they assigned to the various themes. These decisions are reflected, for instance, in the preference for dealing with issues of conflict situations between individual and public needs. In stressing this aspect of the content offered in the unit, teachers may convey to their students implicit messages about life situations in general.

It is generally accepted that teachers act independently behind their classroom doors in choosing instructional strategies for their teaching. What instructional strategies were adopted for teaching this unit? How far did these depart from the strategies suggested in the teachers' guide? The curriculum unit which served as the focus of the study included specific suggestions for instruction. The teachers' guide recommended four instructional strategies. Teacher responses indicated that they used many of these strategies but supplemented them with additional teaching procedures. The strategies recommended in the guide are shown below, together with the frequency of the teachers' statements which referred to these strategies:

1. Classroom discussion   24 percent
2. Reading in classroom based on
   preparatory reading at home   24 percent
3. Individual pupils' use of worksheets   12 percent
4. Group work   12 percent

Other, additional, teaching strategies reported by the teachers included the following: simulation debates between pupils representing different positions, introductory presentation of the topic by the teacher, use of transparencies or other audiovisual methods, presentation of related scientific articles, and oral reports by pupils.

Although it is clear that teachers varied their methods and added their own ideas (eight new ones against the four recommended in the guide), it turns out that relatively little proportional weight was given to the new instructional strategies: 72 percent of the reported references relate to the recommended instructional strategies, and only 28 percent represent new strategies. One may conclude that in this case, although teachers did devise ways of teaching which departed from the developers' suggestions, these were not major elements in their actual teaching.

Sequencing topics and providing links between topics constitute another important element in the planning of instruction. The development team had decided to design the unit as an introduction to the entire course, believing that the specific content would contribute to students' motivation to study botany. However, because the unit is not dependent upon previous knowledge and is not a necessary prerequisite for the following units, its place in the instructional sequence could have been changed by teachers using the materials. Yet all teachers in the study taught the unit as the opening section of the new curriculum topic—the relationship between plants and water. They seemed to have accepted the decisions of curriculum developers regarding the appropriate sequencing of units in the materials. This situation calls to mind Jackson's (1986) statement: "Many teachers never trouble themselves at all with decisions about how the material they are teaching should be presented to their students. Instead, they rely upon commercially prepared instructional materials such as textbooks to make those decisions for them" (Jackson 1986, p. 20).

What reasons were given by the responding teachers for their implementation decisions? Classification of the reasons according to various key words yielded the following breakdown:

1. Roughly half of the reasons cited stemmed from considerations of the attitudes and needs of the pupils: that is, they originated in the teachers' image of the pupils. A third of the teachers described the student popula-

tion as being "disadvantaged" and tended to view this as an important factor influencing their decisions.

2. About a quarter of the reasons cited by teachers stemmed from a consideration of their own attitudes and needs as teachers, such as a personal preference for a certain theme or instructional strategy.

3. Relatively few reasons cited stemmed from a consideration of the instructional objectives as conceived by the teachers. Key phrases here were "It relates to the instructional objectives," "In accordance with a definition of the objectives," or "It is important from a social standpoint." The minor role that objectives play in teachers' decisions about curriculum use conforms to other research findings. (Zahorik 1975)

Teachers' Involvement in Curriculum Implementation

What can we learn from this case about the nature of the involvement of teachers in curriculum implementation? It is one of many cases, and therefore no generalizations are possible. Still, case studies may provide insights into, and raise questions about, cardinal issues of the phenomenon under consideration (Stenhouse 1979).

One of these issues, in the context of the implementation of curriculum materials, is the issue of "fidelity" versus "adaptation." Fullan and Pomfret (1977) speak about different orientations in studies of curriculum implementation. In the framework of the "fidelity" orientation one tends to look for deviations from the original intent of curriculum developers, as reflected in the way the materials are used by teachers. In the framework of an "adaptation" orientation, one tends to look for modifications of curriculum materials according to specific classroom situations. Teachers who taught the unit in botany deviated from the developers' guidelines with respect to time allocation and instructional strategies, although most claimed that they did adhere fully to those guidelines. There seem to exist some ambiguities, and even a measure of dissonance, between teachers' self-image as faithful implementors and their self-declared instructional actions. Teachers' initiative in varying time allocation, and their ingenuity in devising teaching methods beyond those specified in the teachers' guide, may be viewed as an expression of their felt concern for the needs of students in the concrete settings of their classrooms.

One major issue, illuminated by the above study and related to the notion of fidelity versus adaptation, concerns teachers' desire for professional autonomy. Teachers may tend to feel strongly about their autonomy and professional know-how. Lortie (1975) found that many teachers want to add personal aspects to their curricular responsibilities. This sense of autonomy and professionalism may be especially dominant as far as choices of instructional strategies and time allocations are concerned. Teacher autonomy seems to be less pronounced in their treatment of the "educational messages" incorporated in the text of the curriculum materials.

It is our point of view that teachers' adherence to textbooks, teachers' handbooks, and curriculum guidelines is not necessarily a question of lack of inclination to make pedagogical decisions regarding the materials they use. It may be, rather, a question of developing the necessary professional expertise to experiment with the materials. Rudduck (1987) claims that teachers lack the curriculum literacy which is required for the confident critique and adaptation of materials. Teachers seem to restrict themselves mainly to those messages that are explicitly stated in the teachers' guide. Teachers' adherence to the curricular content themes can be interpreted in different ways. One alternative is that teachers prefer to remain faithful to the suggestions included in the guide because they believe that curriculum developers, or authors of commerical textbooks in general, possess valid knowledge and expertise which is reflected in their choice of the topics, themes, and principles included in the materials. Another interpretation of teachers' allegiance to the materials is based on the notion of interpretative abilities. It may be that, lacking adequate training and practice, teachers are not able to elicit additional themes and principles, which may be found in curriculum materials, beyond those that are explicitly mentioned by the developers and authors. A different interpretation may be that the teachers' guide does indeed present teachers with a comprehensive listing of all possible main "educational messages" of the unit, and it is therefore not surprising that the teachers did not exceed the recommendations.

The last alternative is considered to be untenable. It is the main thrust of this book that curriculum materials are richer in educational potential than any predetermined set of intended learning themes and activities stated by the developers. The issue becomes one of the interpretative skills needed for a "reading" of curriculum materials which goes beyond their obvious and explicit meaning. Interpretative skills can be learned and cultivated, leading to an expansion of the repertoire of learning opportunities which teachers offer to their students.

However, teachers may be also constrained in their interpretation of different ways of using the educational potential of materials because of a perception of the authority of the text. A sensed authority and rigidity of curricular texts may inhibit teachers in using the potential richness of existing curriculum materials in a manner which is most appropriate for their students. How to free teachers from the tyranny of curricular texts is the focal point of the following chapters.

As a teacher, administrator, curriculum developer, or curriculum scholar, you may have been involved in the documentation of, and inquiry into, cases of curriculum implementation. You may try to think about such a case and reflect how similar or different it is from the case discussed above. How did teachers allocate time to teaching the various components of the curriculum? Did they go beyond the specific themes suggested in the materials? How varied were their teaching strategies in comparison with those suggested by the curriculum developers? How do you account for some of these commonalities or differences? What may be the impact of the subject matter on the way in which teachers use curriculum materials? And what about the nature of specific students or the background of their teachers? Teachers' varying degrees of mastery of the subject area being taught have been shown to have far-reaching consequences for the complexity of the curricular "stories" they have constructed for their classroom (Gudmunsdottir 1988).

The nature of the materials, whether they are content oriented or process oriented, may determine teachers' use of curriculum materials (Ben-Peretz and Kremer 1979).[2] Treating all innovative curricula in the same way may lead to misinterpretations. For instance, Ben-Peretz and Kremer note that one curriculum package, "The Listening" curriculum, focused on the development of interpersonal communication skills. Because the materials also presented specific literary content, teachers viewed this content as part of the "required learning." The literary examples tend to acquire a significance of their own, which may be counterproductive to the major goals of the innovative curriculum. It seems that a high degree of specification of instructional activities in the materials may lead teachers to emphasize these, sometimes at the expense of providing appropriate experiences for their students.

To sum up this point, it is difficult to generalize across subject matter areas, teachers, and classrooms about modes of teachers' uses of curriculum materials. The implementation case presented herewith is a concrete example of the everyday involvement of teachers in the use of curriculum materials. This case raised several issues, among them the issue of teacher autonomy and the issue of the potential diversity of educational themes or "messages" embodied in curriculum texts.

TEACHERS AS CURRICULUM DEVELOPERS

Up to this point we have discussed a case of teachers' involvement in curriculum implementation. We turn now to a case of another kind of curriculum function of teachers, namely, teachers' role in curriculum development (Ben-Peretz 1980a). Teachers participate from time to time in curriculum development efforts, whether school based or centrally organized. Sometimes teachers are involved in the construction of curriculum guides, but more often their contribution lies in the preparation of curriculum materials for classroom use. Different modes of teachers' involvement as developers may affect the nature of the curriculum materials on the one hand, and the anticipated use of these materials by other teachers on the other hand. The purpose of presenting the following case of curriculum development by teachers is twofold: (1) to discuss a possible function of teachers in the curriculum domain; and (2) to demonstrate a link between teachers as curriculum developers and teachers as users and implementors of curriculum materials.

Teachers may be viewed as "instruments" for achieving the intentions of curriculum developers. This approach may be powerful in limiting teachers' motivation for curriculum change and adaptation. Their role may be compared to the role of performing musicians who are bound by the score of composers. Musicians may present their own interpretations of a composition, but they are not expected to rewrite it. In the curricular approach that guided the development project described herewith, teachers were perceived as creators of the curriculum, composers of their own "music." Their knowledge of subject matter and classrooms, their concerns, and their needs became the starting point of the curricular process. Teachers' expertise about classroom reality was the basis for discerning practical problems that call for curricular remedies. Westbury (1972) characterized Schwab's (1969) approach to the practical mode of curriculum work as drawing upon "an image of a creative and practical reformer discerning problems through an awareness of apparent gaps between what should be and what is, then seeking solutions from his understanding of what might be done, and finally moving to bring about change or improvement" (p. 30). Because teachers are familiar with classroom situations, their role is deemed central for discovering these gaps and bringing about change or improvement. Teachers know their learners, classrooms, and school milieu in a way that central curriculum developers can never know. This knowledge enables teachers to reveal weaknesses, shortcomings, and conditions which should and can be changed. The perception of teachers as sensitive to, and knowledgeable about, problem situations in school demands their being assigned a central role in the curriculum process that starts with the locating of curricular problems (Schwab 1983). The question arises whether teachers have the necessary expertise in curriculum development and the construction of materials.

Several kinds of knowledge are important for the task of curriculum revision: knowledge of the discipline to be taught, knowledge about the nature of learners, knowledge of the context of school reality and of the community at large, knowledge of the characteristics of the teachers who are going to use the curricular materials, and knowledge of the curriculum-making process itself (Schwab 1973). Two or more of the required kinds of knowledge may be found in one person. In the curriculum development case presented here, teachers were considered to represent knowledge of learners, teachers, and school milieu. In the development process, teachers were assisted by subject matter specialists and by experts in curriculum development. Fox (1972) comments upon the controlling role usually played by subject matter specialists: "Educators, even those who are confident and creative in the classroom, are often awed and thus paralyzed by the subject matter specialist" (p. 71). In order to overcome this effect, experts in the curriculum development process described here were not regular members of the development team but fulfilled their role in development as external advisors. Thus the possible tendency of teachers to subordinate their own ideas to those of specialists was largely avoided. When experts are not part of the regular deliberations of the planning team, their advice can be sought whenever the developers need it. The recommendations of experts are then considered by the teacher-developers, who may accept or reject them. In the specific case reported here, a curriculum expert acted as chairperson of the development team, organizing and administering its work.

So far we have treated two guiding principles of this mode of curriculum development:teachers served as the starting point in defining problems and aims for curricular deliberations, and experts acted in an advisory capacity only and not as members of the development team. We turn now to the third principle guiding the development project: the modular nature of the curriculum materials which were the product of the development process.

The end product of the development process in this case was not one "package" of curriculum materials but rather a number of different modules. All the modules dealt with the same topic but differed in specific content, style of presentation, and choice of instructional strategies. This format was adopted because of its congruence with the central role assigned to teachers in the development process. Teachers who become members of a development team may have different backgrounds, different orientations to subject matter and instruction, different teaching experiences, and different educational priorities. Their divergent viewpoints may find their expression in the variety of suggestions made in the course of curriculum construction. Because of the deliberate lack of pressure for early closure and for consensus about the nature and format of the materials, the curricular product is in the form of a number of modular units, representing different approaches to the same subject matter topic. The modular format of materials provides maximum flexibility and openness for teachers who are involved in the decision-making process. Moreover, the pluralistic nature of the curriculum product, which consists of alternative versions of the same topic, may release teachers, who will act as implementors of these materials, from dependence on the intentions of curriculum developers. Teachers who encounter diverse curricular options bearing on the same topic, all of which were developed by their peers, may see themselves free to choose among these options. Alternatively, they may decide to combine different components of each of these versions, and thus create their own set of curriculum materials. Carrying this process one step further, teachers may be motivated to develop a completely different version based on their own knowledge, instructional preferences, and insights into the nature of their teaching situation.

Let us return to the description of the development project. Six teachers were members of the development team. They were selected because of their previous success in teaching and their comprehensive subject matter knowledge. All were experienced teachers who came from different schools, urban and rural, serving high- and low-level socioeconomic populations. The unit chosen for the project was part of a biology curriculum "Man in Nature" by Ben-Peretz et al.; (see Curriculum Materials following References).* The unit itself deals with the "Uniqueness of Man," focusing on the nervous system. The "Uniqueness of Man" project was carried out with the support of the Ministry of Education. Teachers received special payment for their work on the project. This was one way of demonstrating the official recognition of the importance of teachers' involvement in curriculum development. School administrators, such as supervisors in biology, were invited to participate in the deliberations of the team. School principals supported the participation of their teachers in the project. The overall message of these administrative arrangements was that curriculum development by teachers was considered to be an accepted and viable strategy for curriculum development.

The Curriculum Development Process

Initial deliberations and choices

As a start in their curricular deliberations, teachers were asked to offer suggestions about the specific topics and instructional strategies which should be included in the curriculum materials. Teachers made different suggestions and did not agree on content or on instructional strategies. The diversity of views may be explained in a number of ways: teachers had different areas of interest; some preferred ethology, whereas others focused on molecular biology. Teachers differed in their educational experiences; some came from middle-class schools, and some taught mainly disadvantaged students. Their educational philosophies and orientations toward teaching varied; some preferred learning by discovery methods, whereas others thought that expository teaching would be more appropriate. It may be assumed that such differences exist as well among teachers who are potential users of any

---

* Hereafter references to curriculum materials will be signified by *CM*.

kind of ready-made curriculum materials. These individual differences have to be taken into consideration in the implementation process of the materials.

The first planning meetings were devoted to preliminary discussions about suggestions made by teachers. In spite of differences of opinion, the common tendency among the participants was to try to arrive at a consensus about a content and mode of instruction which would be acceptable to all. This tendency was contrary to the intention of constructing a curriculum product consisting of alternative versions for the teachers who may use the materials. Several possible reasons may account for the perceived tendency of teachers to arrive at a consensus about educational purposes and at a common curricular approach. Teachers might be unfamiliar with a situation in which the choice of curriculum materials was in the hands of teachers. Some found it difficult to give up the notion that complete coverage of different aspects of the subject matter is a basic requirement for learning any scientific topic. They found it hard to accept a strategy of developing an alternative curricular version that would portray partial views of the subject matter being taught. Teachers' need for complete coverage of subject matter topics in schools has already been mentioned as one of the concerns teachers have regarding the curriculum they teach. Teachers also considered the construction of alternative versions an unrealistic effort which would be too costly and time-consuming. Subject matter experts as well as educators joined the deliberations at this point. Both the subject matter experts and the educators convinced the team that it was indeed possible to construct alternative versions without distorting the subject matter and without misrepresenting it to students. Four different versions of the materials were therefore decided on:

1. An anatomical-morphological version, focusing on the anatomical-morphological differences between humans and animals. In this version the uniqueness of mankind is perceived as relating to specific behavior, especially manual dexterity and language skills. This version offered a variety of student activities, such as visits to the zoo.

2. A physiological version, based to a large extent on comprehension of text, emphasizing physiological characteristics of the human nervous system.

3. A psychological version, concentrating on the unique learning and thinking abilities of mankind. This version presents students with many opportunities for experimentation.
4. A programmed version for individual learning, dealing with basic terms and concepts relating to the nervous system.

Each version represents a different aspect of content and choice of instructional strategies. The participating teachers agreed that all versions should stress the distinctive human features of mankind.

Preliminary construction of materials

Subteams of teachers were set up according to areas of interest. Each subteam was responsible for constructing one curricular version. Work in small groups was considered essential for the process. Individual work provides fewer opportunities for the exchange of ideas and lacks the kind of group spirit which seems to be rewarding to teachers involved in the curriculum development project. For technical reasons there was a time that one teacher worked by herself. This proved to be an unproductive situation as far as the creative process of curriculum construction was concerned. It seems that a subteam of two developers is the "critical mass" for teachers cooperating in curriculum development. Cooperation among teachers is considered to contribute to the effectiveness in finding solutions to educational problems. Lortie (1975) states, "Relationships among teachers may deepen and broaden. Considerable effort is being expended today to foster closer working relationships among teachers" (p. 209). Teachers' experiences in collaboration in development projects may be productive for preparing them for varied further cooperative efforts in school. Such cooperation may be also valuable in joint attempts to adapt curriculum materials to local school situations.

During the stage of preliminary construction of materials, teachers were assisted by subject matter experts and by the chairperson of the development group.

Teachers started the writing process by devising activities for students. The advantages of starting the curriculum construction process by listing possible learning activities and of relating these to potential learning outcomes at a later stage were conceived as twofold. First, teachers have intimate experience and knowledge about teaching strategies, and in starting from planning activities they were given the opportunity to draw upon their special expertise and professional strength. Second, when planning their lessons, the question "What should I do in my own classroom tomorrow?" is usually foremost in teachers' minds. Teachers who started with this question in their development groups were thus given an opportunity to start their planning on the basis of their own professional needs.

Research on teachers' planning shows that teachers tend to focus on student activities and content decisions. Teachers apparently spend the smallest proportion of their planning efforts on the specification of objectives (Zahorik 1975; Peterson, Marx, and Clark 1978). Teachers who participated in the curriculum project worked in a manner which was consistent with the preferred mode of teacher planning. The curriculum materials constructed by them may therefore be more helpful for other teachers. The learning activities were chosen by the teachers according to the following criteria: appropriateness for student target population, feasibility for classroom use, and the personal priorities and preferences of the teachers.

Trial uses

The trial use of tentative parts of curriculum materials is an important stage in curriculum construction. The participating teachers used the materials in their own classrooms and noted their impressions of students' reactions to the materials. Concurrently subject matter experts were asked to evaluate the materials. The data collected in the first trial use of the materials were the basis for further group deliberations and for rewriting. Further decisions were made about content, instructional strategies, and activities. The possible learning outcomes of the various activities were considered, and those considered most appropriate were included in the published trial editions of the materials.

The final rewriting and editing was done by the subteams assisted by the chairperson, editors, and illustrators. Each subteam was fully responsible for the complete task of preparing the materials, working in the framework of financial constraints and other practical pressures such as time limits.

The trial editions were submitted to formal trial runs carried out by teachers who were not part of the development team. These teachers participated in a special in-service program planned and conducted by the members of the team. The in-service teacher program was guided by an image of teachers as adaptors of materials and as flexible implementors. The characteristics of the training program were therefore as follows:

1. The curriculum product presented to teachers was in a modular format composed of four different versions, as opposed to one obligatory curriculum package. Teachers' encounter with varied materials all dealing with the same topic provided opportunities for considering appropriate choices.

2. Protocols of developers' deliberations were offered as part of the in-service program. Providing teachers with the rationale of the developers and the basis for their curricular decisions permitted teachers to question those decisions and to draw their own conclusions about the materials. Rudduck (1987) draws attention to the importance of sharing with practitioners the inside story of curriculum development: "An understanding of the dilemmas that shaped the process of creation is the pre-condition of intelligent experimentation" (p. 87).

3. No teachers' guide or manual was presented to teachers. The initiative for the use of the materials was left in the hands of teachers. They offered their own suggestions about the adaptation of learner activities, the sequence of topics, and such matters.

Special strategies were devised to foster teacher autonomy and flexibility in the implementation of the materials. Teachers participating in the in-service program were asked to propose a variety of ways for teaching the unit "Uniqueness of Man." All their suggestions were listed and discussed. Some of their proposals were similar to the alternatives chosen by the teacher-developers, and some were different. Teachers in the training program became sensitive to the variety of approaches that might be adopted in the construction of curricular materials related to one specific topic. They became aware of the complex issues involved in the process of developing the unit. Through their own explorations they became involved in the process and were motivated to try out different combinations of the materials. The teachers who had participated in the in-service program then tried the materials in their classes. On the basis of the evaluation of these trial runs, the final edition was produced by the same teachers who were involved in the curriculum development process from its first stage.

After reading about the case of teacher involvement in curriculum development, it may be of interest to compare this case with your own experiences in curriculum development. You may ask yourself who the participants in the process were, what the role of subject matter experts was, and what the nature of the end product was. Was the developmental effort confined to the boundaries of one school, or was it intended to serve wider audiences? How were teachers expected to use the materials, and how, if at all, were they introduced to the curriculum? What do you consider to be the advantages and the drawbacks of either development mode? What are some of the implications for curriculum use in classrooms? You may wish to become engaged in curriculum development and to try the described mode of development.

Teachers' Involvement in Curriculum Development

What can we learn from the reported case about teacher involvement in curriculum development? Several issues are evoked. First and foremost, teacher involvement in curriculum development is a lengthy and costly process. Teachers who participate in the process need ample time for their development activities. They need formal recognition of the educational establishment and the professional support of a curriculum consultant. The specific organizational arrangements may depend on the anticipated use of the materials. In the case described above, the materials were meant to be implemented beyond the classrooms of the developers. This was not a case of school-based curriculum development, but rather a case of teacher involvement in the "external" process of curriculum development, carried out by agencies outside the schools. Still, it is contended that even in the context of the development of curriculum materials for one school, or even for one classroom, teachers who act as developers need time, resources, and professional support.

Another emerging issue concerns the search for new formats of curriculum materials based on teachers' preferences and perceptions. The multiple modules which were constructed in the described case are just examples of the wide variety of curricular possibilities that exist once teachers function as initiators of the process. Manifold possible formats may be more responsive to the actual needs of learners in diverse classroom situations.

The construction of curriculum materials is viewed as a cooperative effort demanding close collaboration and sharing. It may well be that all forms of teacher-curriculum encounters, as users and innovators, would benefit from this mode of cooperation and sharing. Teachers could become curriculum developers in a variety of educational contexts. They could function as grass-roots developers in their schools, preparing curriculum units for use in their own classrooms. Teachers could also construct alternative local versions of existing materials, extending their uses through appropriate modifications for specific teaching situations. The in-service training which was part of the project emphasized active involvement in curricular deliberations, even when these were carried out after the actual development process had been terminated. The opportunity to discuss with one's colleagues the nature of materials and their possible classroom uses is seen as a prerequisite for flexible and adaptive curriculum implementation.

Have you been party to such discussions? How were these conducted? You may wish to initiate such discussions in your own school.

At this point in our discussion the two cases described here, one related to teachers as implementors and one concerning teachers as developers, intersect. Curriculum development by teachers may be meant for other teachers, but these do not have to be faithful implementors of the ideas which originated elsewhere. Schwab (1983) puts it in the following way: "It [the curriculum] is not decided in Moscow and telegraphed to the provinces" (p. 240). The implementing teachers are perceived as full partners in the development process, shaping the finished product according to their own needs, adapting it to their own teaching circumstances. Curricular abilities acquired through participation in development projects could serve teachers in the implementation of externally developed curriculum materials, including commercially prepared textbooks. Awareness of curricular deliberations and choices could enhance teachers' ability to function as autonomous decision makers. It is "important to find ways of inviting teachers into the world of deliberation that the curriculum developers inhabited so that they would, to some extent, be able to reconstruct the process of development; in this way they would be in a better position to respond critically to the product" (Rudduck 1987, p. 81). This view calls for a new process of teacher involvement in the curriculum realm. Some components of this process have been presented here. The whole issue will be treated in greater depth in the following chapters.

CONCLUDING COMMENTS

This chapter has focused on a detailed description and analysis of teachers acting as curriculum users and as curriculum creators. The complexity of both functions is highlighted, and the professional requirements related to curricular issues are clarified. Teachers are called upon to reflect on their own activities in the light of these cases.

RECOMMENDED ADDITIONAL READINGS

Several books and articles on curriculum use by teachers may serve to expand your view of this process. Among them are the following:

Fullan, M. (1982): *The Meaning of Educational Change*, Toronto, OISE Press.

Fullan, M., and Pomfret, A. (1977. "Research on curriculum and instruction implementation," *Review of Educational Research* 47, 1:335–397.

Leithwood, K., and MacDonald, R. (1981). "Decisions given by teachers for their curriculum choices," *Canadian Journal of Education* 6, 2:103–116.

McLaughlin, M., and Marsh, D. (1978): "Staff development and school change," *Teachers College Record* 80, 1:69–94.

Sarason, S. (1982): *The Culture of School and the Problem of Change*, Boston, Allyn and Bacon: 1st edition 1971.

Divergent cases of the process of curriculum development in different contexts are described and analyzed in the following books and articles:

Kennedy, K. J., and McDonald, G. (1986): "Designing curriculum materials for multicultural education. Lessons from an Australian Development Project," *Curriculum Inquiry* 16, 3:311–326.

Reid, W. D., and Walker, D. F. (eds.) (1975): *Case Studies on Curriculum Change*, London, Routledge and Kegan Paul.

Shipman, M. D., Bolam, D., and Jenkins, D. R. (1974): *Inside a Curriculum Project: A Case Study in the Process of Curriculum Change*, London, Methuen.

Stenhouse, L. (ed.) (1980): *Curriculum Research and Development in Action*, London, Heineman.

Walker, D. F. (1974): "A naturalistic model for curriculum development," *School Review* 79, 1:51–65.

School-based curriculum development constitutes a special mode of teacher involvement in the curriculum domain. The following are some relevant writings in this area:

Sabar, N., Rudduck, J., and Reid, W. A. (1987): *Partnership and Autonomy in School-based Curriculum Development*, USDE Papers in Education, University of Sheffield.

Skilbeck, M. (1984): *School-based Curriculum Development*, London, Harper and Row.

2

Coping with Curriculum

"If at first you don't succeed,
blame it on the teacher"
Paul Dickson, The Official Rules, *1978, p. 16*

The two cases studies presented in the first chapter portrayed possible forms of teacher involvement with curriculum issues: teachers as implementors of externally prepared materials and as creators of their own curriculum materials. We turn now to a more detailed analysis of teachers' ways of coping with curriculum issues and the problems they face.

The use of curriculum materials is an essential part of the professional activities of all teachers. The ways in which teachers handle the curriculum determine, to a large extent, the learning processes in their classrooms. Several questions ensue from this proposition: How do we define curriculum? Which are the specific kinds of curriculum materials which teachers encounter in their school practice? What are the different professional activities of teachers related to the curriculum they use or construct?

DEFINITIONS

What do we mean by the term *curriculum*? Traditionally *curriculum* means a course of studies. Over the years curriculum theorists have suggested a variety of definitions. One view limits the concept of curriculum to a list of intended learning outcomes (Johnson 1967). Another, comprehensive, view defines *curriculum* as the whole set of experiences learners have under the guidance of schools (Oliver 1977). A distinction may be made between curriculum plans and instructional plans. Some educators claim that the development of both curriculum plans, focusing on choice of content and determination of goals, and instructional plans, focusing on suggested learning strategies, should be left to curriculum developers. Robinsohn (1969), for instance, sees curriculum devel-

23

opment as "the construction and revision of ordered sequences of learning experiences related to intended objectives" (p. 221). According to this view, teachers are responsible for the implementation of externally planned sequences of instruction. On the other hand, Johnson (1967) argues that the planning of instruction based on external curriculum plans has to be in the hands of teachers, because they are the ones who know the nature of their specific classrooms. These different positions may have far-reaching implications for the anticipated encounter between teachers and curriculum, as well as for curricular practices that are found in the educational system. It is maintained here that teachers have a dominant impact on the implementation of *any* form of curriculum, even if this includes detailed specifications of instruction. Still, different forms of curricula and different role expectations of teachers may lead to significant variations in curriculum use. Let us imagine a teacher who is free to choose from a variety of textbooks and whose teaching is guided only by curricular guidelines which define the content to be taught. This teacher will have to be more active in choices and planning than a teacher who is expected to implement a curriculum "package" which includes precise instructional materials and detailed guides for teachers.

A conception of curriculum which emphasizes the central role of teachers was stipulated by Schwab (1983): "Curriculum is what is successfully conveyed to differing degrees to different students, by committed teachers using appropriate materials and actions, of legitimated bodies of knowledge, skill, taste, and propensity to act and react, which are chosen for instruction after serious reflection and communal decision by representatives of those involved in the teaching of a specified group of students who are known to the decision makers" (p. 240). In this approach to curriculum, teachers are central figures in a number of ways. Teachers' knowledge and experience with students are crucial for making valid curricular decisions. In Schwab's own words, "teachers must be involved in debate, deliberation, and decision about what and how to teach" (p. 245). A curriculum is viewed as the learning experiences shaped by committed teachers for their own students who use appropriate materials and actions in their classrooms. This view of curriculum serves as the basis for the approach to the teacher-curriculum encounter elaborated in this book. The first case described in Chapter 1 was an example of teachers' involvement as users of materials, devising instructional actions. The second case represents teachers' involvement in curriculum "debate" and "deliberation."

CURRICULUM FORMS

What are some of the actual and concrete forms of curriculum materials in the everyday context of schools? From this point of view curricula may appear in a variety of forms, guises, or even disguises. "Curriculum disguises" are those forms of materials which do not appear at first sight to represent school curricula. For instance, tests and external examinations may be viewed as a curriculum in "disguise." External examinations may determine the choice of teaching topics and teaching modes without bearing the formal title of "curriculum." If, for instance, examinations in biology include "hands-on" experimentation, teachers may tend to focus on experiments in their classes.

The most common forms of curriculum teachers encounter in their work are the following:

1. A syllabus—lists of specified content. Syllabi may include the rationale for choices of content items, as well as specified intended learning outcomes and suggestions about allocation of time to the various topics.
2. Teacher handbooks or guidelines. These usually include details about the topics to be taught, predetermined teaching goals and suggestions for instructional strategies.
3. Textbooks, which may be the product of the teamwork of a curriculum development project or written by individual authors for commercial publishers.
4. Additional instructional materials, such as worksheets, films, tapes, and so forth.
5. Materials for student assessment, tests, and other kinds of examination modes, such as questionnaires measuring attitudes toward specific subject matter areas.
6. A comprehensive "curriculum package" consisting of teachers' guidebooks, student textbooks, audiovisual material, and tests.
7. Scientific texts or literary texts, which may become the "curriculum" used by teachers.
8. Curriculum materials developed by the teachers themselves. Sometimes even their students, or their students' parents, may be involved in this process.

Each of these forms will be viewed as a representation of *curriculum* in the context of classrooms.

We turn now to a more detailed description of several common curriculum forms. The first to be described is the *syllabus*, which is usually defined as "a course of study" or "a program defining document" (Popham 1975). The syllabus may present the obligatory content of a course, specifying its sequence and estimated time allocations. Sometimes the syllabus is transformed into a more elaborate document that reflects the educational rationale of its authors. Ministry guidelines for teachers are examples of such elaborated syllabi. *Guidelines* may include the rationale of their developers, elaborated descriptions of goals and objectives, and detailed specifications of the content to be covered. Sometimes guidelines contain suggestions for teaching strategies. Since syllabi and guidelines are written in different styles and formats, bearing explicit and implicit messages, the process of interpreting these documents may be extremely complex and even problematic. It should not surprise us, therefore, that teachers may claim that guidelines do not tell them what to do in their classrooms. Student teachers, for instance, may find such guidelines extremely confusing:

> The math lessons, they're so short, it says like objective—
> "to get the kids to know about representing length"—
> Okay, what's that supposed to mean? And it says, "you'll
> need these materials"—Okay, I've got the materials, now
> what am I supposed to do with them? . . . You know, it
> doesn't hardly tell you anything . . . I am not sure what
> they mean by all this stuff? (Loewenberg-Ball and Feiman-
> Nemser 1988, p. 416)

The obvious question to raise is whether the function of syllabi and teacher guidelines should, or could be, to "tell teachers what to do," or whether syllabi and guidelines should be viewed as stimuli for teachers' creative planning of their lessons.

Teachers also encounter curriculum in the form of prepared *packages* of *commercial materials*. These may consist of textbooks, teacher handbooks, and instructional aids, such as films or worksheets. Sometimes the materials include sets of tests for student evaluation and even forms for teachers' self-evaluation. *English Alpha*, edited by Kenton Sutherland (CM—1982), is a good example of such a comprehensive curriculum package. *English Alpha* consists of six textbooks for teaching English as a second language.

The student text is accompanied by a comprehensive teachers' guide. This guide lists teaching goals (such as new communication skills), the key ideas of each unit (such as the nature of passive verbs), and suggestions for teaching (such as having students work in groups of three, asking each other questions). Test forms, anticipated answers, and record-keeping charts are also part of the teachers' edition. Supplementary materials are provided and consist of practice workbooks for students and casette tapes.

Sometimes teachers use curriculum which is in the form of scholarly materials, *scientific texts*, or *literary texts*. Teachers attempting to base their teaching on these materials use their understanding of the subject matter, be it biology or literature, to transform them for instruction. From teachers' points of view there is a significant difference between original scientific or literary texts, which they may use in their teaching, and specifically constructed curriculum materials. Use of the first kind of material demands complex subject matter knowledge and pedagogical experience. Inexperienced teachers, with a limited repertoire of teaching strategies and routines, may find the task of "transformation" formidable (Borko et al. 1988). It is argued that knowing different ways of teaching a specific subject matter area constitutes part of the "pedagogical content knowledge" of experienced teachers (Shulman 1986; Gudmunsdottir and Shulman 1986). In further chapters issues of transformation of such resources into learning experiences will be discussed.

As mentioned, teachers may devise *their own curriculum*, sometimes involving their students in the process. This, too, is a form of curriculum, though not prescribed by external authorities, not even by the school itself. Butt et al. (1986) quote a teacher who describes his own curriculum in geography for the ninth grade:

> The options I teach are open and I develop the curriculum completely on my perception of how the students can most readily learn those things I think they should know from the course. This freedom to develop allows me to do things in more unorthodox ways. Students build tests, they develop information sheets, they teach classes, they make and play games and they build and demonstrate models. They participate more directly in the curriculum building process. (p. 318)

It is interesting to note how this teacher actually involves the students in the process of curriculum development.

Which forms of "curriculum" are you familiar with, and which forms are prevalent in your own classroom? Try to list some advantages and disadvantages of each form. You may wish to discuss your list with your colleagues.

CURRICULAR DISTINCTIONS

A number of curricular distinctions are relevant at this point. The first is the distinction between *mandated* and *open* (self-initiated) curricula. In their professional activities teachers may be required to implement a mandated curriculum, imposed by agents which are external to the classroom. Mandated curricula, as distinguished from open curricula, may exist in varied forms. Their sources may be distant, such as the ministry of education or the school board, or close by, such as the principal's office. Implementation may be anticipated to adhere closely to the intentions of the developers, in line with a fidelity implementation approach, or, conversely, adaptations may be called for. What is common to all mandated curricula is that their initiation and development are not in the hands of the teachers themselves, as is the case with the open, self-initiated curriculum exemplified in Chapter 1 and in the above quote from Butt et al. (1986).

Another distinction considered to be meaningful for teachers is that between *structured, sequential* and *unstructured, modular* curriculum materials. Different forms of curriculum materials, guidelines, or fully developed curriculum packages may possess a structured character and may exhibit an inherent sequential hierarchy of topics and learning experiences. The *English Alpha* curriculum is an example of the structured, sequential curriculum form. On the other hand, curriculum materials may be modular and unstructured, allowing for flexible use and different modes of sequencing, like the "Uniqueness of Man" materials described in Chapter 1.

The distinction between *detailed* and *general* forms of curriculum materials and the implications for teachers were mentioned above. Teachers who use guidelines that do not include detailed suggestions about sequences, time allocations, and instructional strategies have to depend more on their own planning. This situation requires special kinds of curricular literacy, which will be discussed further on.

Another curricular distinction is related to the anticipated *period of teaching time* covered by curriculum materials, which may be long or relatively short. In Chapter 1 we saw an example of a unit which was intended for two lesson periods only. On the other hand, the *English Alpha* materials cover beginning, intermediate, and advanced levels of English, and are intended for a long teaching period. Clark and Yinger (1979) found that teachers may use incremental or comprehensive strategies in planning their lessons. Incremental planning depends on relatively short steps and relies on day-to-day classroom information. Comprehensive planning constitutes elaborated and specified frameworks for future action. The match or mismatch between the nature of curriculum materials and the planning style of teachers has to be considered and may shape the nature of the teacher-curriculum encounter.

Thus far, some definitions and distinctions that may be relevant to teachers have been presented, and some possible problems and concerns related to these have been raised. These distinctions are considered important for teachers involved in curriculum development and use. Teachers may approach curricula differently according to these distinctions. For instance, some teachers may prefer mandated curricula, whereas others may feel professionally limited unless they initiate and create their own curricula. Curriculum characteristics may be perceived as constraining or, conversely, as liberating teacher action. For instance, some teachers may feel that the predetermined structure and sequence of a textbook help them in their teaching, whereas others may need the freedom for flexible sequencing, even when using mandated curricula. Teachers who are aware of these distinctions may become more reflective in their practice, whether they implement externally prepared materials or create their own.

You may wish to sort the curriculum materials that you use regularly according to the curricular distinctions presented here. Which kinds of materials are you most comfortable with? What are some educational meanings of these distinctions for your own teaching? Which characteristics would you choose in your own curriculum planning?

Let us turn now to some concrete examples of teachers' activities coping with everyday curricular issues and problems.

THE CURRICULAR ACTIVITIES OF TEACHERS

The following are some vignettes which represent possible teacher activities in different curricular contexts. Let us start with Helen's story:

Helen teaches literature in the ninth grade of a junior high school. She is an experienced teacher and loves literature. Lately she has become concerned about "the decline of moral standards of youth," as she puts it. Examining the list of books in her syllabus, she asks herself, "Why was this book included in the syllabus? Which values can be articulated and clarified through studying it?" Helen claims, "If I don't find satisfying answers to these questions, I won't choose the specific book for my teaching."

In this case Helen is engaged in acting as a *curriculum choice maker*. She applies her own principles and criteria in order to reach decisions about the specific curriculum content she will teach. Several issues may determine teachers' curricular choices. Often, time constraints (number of lessons per week, or necessary preparation time for teachers) have a strong impact on teachers' choices.

Lack of time is a persistent problem in school. The lack of time forces teachers to make choices. For instance, teachers may be bothered by the issue of "coverage," the need to choose between breadth versus depth in teaching any subject matter area. They may ask themselves whether to try to cover every content item in the textbook. In the first chapter this issue was mentioned in the context of curriculum development by teachers. Coverage is a recurring problem in many encounters between teachers and curriculum. It is important to deal with it explicitly while preparing teachers for curriculum use. There does not seem to be a clear-cut general answer; therefore, teachers have to cope with it on the basis of a comprehensive understanding of the nature of the curriculum on the one hand, and their teaching situation on the other. We shall return to this issue later.

Choosing which components of the curriculum to focus on and which level of exhaustiveness to prefer is not the only professional activity of teachers regarding the curriculum, as is demonstrated in the following vignette:

John is a biology teacher in high school, and has used the same textbook for several years. He is tired of the same text, the same experiments, the same questions and answers; "I feel like someone who is sentenced to fulfill an unchanging constant role in a bad play. I would like to change the script." John found that the textbook presentation of Mendel's basic issues of genetics was dry and that many of his students found the materials difficult. He decided to replace the text with portions of Mendel's nineteenth century original paper. The focus of his teaching changed. Classroom discussions dealt with the nature of communication between scientists and with the personal history of some scientists, like Mendel, whose contributions to science were recognized only after their death. John's students learned about Mendel's laws, but they also learned about the social context of scientific endeavors.

In this case John can be described as a *curriculum adaptor*, who changes parts of the curriculum materials in response to the perceived needs of his students and in line with his own interests. Fullan (1982) mentions the tremendous power teachers have to introduce any changes they see appropriate in the process of curriculum implementation. Teachers' adaptation of curriculum and their attempts to introduce changes in existing texts raise the problem of adherence to curricular guidelines or to curriculum materials. How far may teachers go in their adaptations without destroying the spirit and meaning of the curriculum they implement in their classes?

This question may be a genuine concern of curriculum developers and teachers. For instance, developers may have constructed curriculum materials for specific situations, such as teaching in extremely heterogeneous classes. Teachers who introduce too many changes into these materials may cause distortions rather than accommodate them to the needs of their students. The notion of a 'curriculum envelope' may be helpful in dealing with this problem; Bridgham (1971) suggests that new curricula are like "trajectories through pedagogic space." They are "properly defined not by single lines in that space but rather by envelopes containing an infinite set of allowed solutions to the problems, envisaged by the curriculum designers" (p. 64). The boundaries of curricular envelopes may be conceived as consisting of certain general characteristics chosen by the developers. These characteristics may concern specific content or instructional strategies. A set of biology curriculum materials, for instance, may be characterized by an emphasis on concepts of evolution or on adopting instructional methods of active discovery. Curriculum analysis may help teachers to discriminate between changes in the text which are "inside" or "outside" the curriculum envelope. Teachers may decide to restrict their modifications to changes inside the limits of the curriculum envelope, keeping its major features. On the other hand, teachers may decide to go beyond the boundaries of the curriculum and modify even its main characteristics. For instance, experimentation with live organisms may be a central feature of a biology curriculum. Teachers who find that they object to such experimentation on moral grounds may devise other modes of teaching the same content. Curriculum analysis may help teachers to recognize the special characteristics of curriculum materials. Such insights may aid teachers in their efforts to interpret materials and to plan their lessons on the basis of this interpretation. Several modes of curriculum analysis will be discussed further on.

You may try to determine the specific characteristics of your own curriculum in the area you teach. What do you consider valid and defensible reasons for moving "outside" your curriculum? Try to think of some concrete examples of your curricular decisions which led to far-reaching changes in the curriculum you use. An interesting discussion may ensue if you compare your own decisions with those of your colleagues.

Sometimes the introduction of changes into existing curriculum materials, such as textbooks, is not enough, and teachers undertake the *creation of their own curricula*. Teacher-based curriculum development may be called forth for a number of reasons. Special needs of student groups may require individualized curriculum materials which are not to be found commercially. The faculty of a school may decide to try to react to some societal problems, such as a high incidence of teenage pregnancies, through the local development of a course on family life and family planning. Because of the great sensitivity of such issues, it is necessary to bear in mind the specific beliefs and values of students, parents, and community while constructing such a course. This kind of teacher-based curriculum development is different from the case described in Chapter 1, which was part of the centralized curriculum effort of the Ministry of Education. On the other hand, local projects may be intended for one class or one school. Such school-based curriculum development (SBCD) may cover a whole school curriculum, or be confined to one or more school subjects, or to even one topic or theme.[3] There is no doubt that teachers need special professional skills to fulfill the role of school-based curriculum developers, skills which have to be learned and practiced.

CONCLUDING COMMENTS

Various definitions of the term *curriculum* were offered in this chapter. Schwab's (1983) conception of curriculum as the comprehensive educational experiences planned for specified groups of students and emphasizing teachers' crucial role in the process served as the conceptual basis for the main theses of this book. Curricular forms which are part of the professional environment of teachers were noted and discussed.

Different contexts in which teachers are required to perform curricular tasks were described, and different kinds of curricular activities were mentioned. Teachers make curricular choices, and they adapt and mold existing curriculum materials to their specific teaching situations. Sometimes teachers are involved in the construction of their own curriculum, but mostly they are engaged in the implementation of curriculum materials which were developed outside the schools in which they teach. One may claim that curricular issues play a major part in the everyday professional activities of teachers at all grade levels.

The centrality of curriculum in teachers' lives leads to the following question: What concerns do teachers have about their involvement in the curriculum and the variety of curricular activities they perform?

RECOMMENDED ADDITIONAL READINGS

The following writings may be useful for thinking about ways in which teachers approach curriculum issues in their classrooms:

Connelly, F. M., and Clandinin, D. J. (1988): *Teachers as Curriculum Planners: Narratives of Experience*, New York, Teachers College Press, and Toronto, OISE Press.

Connelly, F. M., and Elbaz, F. (1980): "Conceptual bases for curriculum thought: A teacher's perspective," in A. W. Foshay, (ed.), *Considered Action for Curriculum Improvement*, Washington D.C., Association for Supervision and Curriculum Development, pp. 95–119.

Elbaz, F. (1983): *Teacher Thinking: A Study of Practical Knowledge*, London, Croom Helm.

3

Teachers' Concerns
about Curriculum Issues

"The world is more complicated than
most of our theories make it out to be"
Paul Dickson, The Official Rules, *1978, p. 12*

In Chapters 1 and 2 we discussed a variety of curricular functions
and activities of teachers in different situations, as choice makers,
adaptors, or creators of curriculum materials. It was argued that
teachers need special qualifications and expertise for carrying out
these functions. Before elaborating on the nature of these qualifications, let us ask ourselves what we, as teachers, think about our
curricular functions. How do we perceive our curricular roles?
And what concerns do we have about our professional activities
related to the curriculum? The identification of such concerns and
perceptions may help us to gain insights into the ways in which
teachers tend to use or to devise curriculum materials. Such insights may also serve the creation of a framework for greater
teacher autonomy in teachers' encounters with curriculum.

WHAT TEACHERS WANT TO KNOW ABOUT
CURRICULUM MATERIALS

We start with some findings on teachers' concerns about curriculum issues which are based on research conducted by Ben-Peretz
and Tamir (1981). Several problems were investigated in this
study. The investigators wanted to find out how teachers view
their own role in curriculum implementation and whether this
view is congruent with an image of teachers as autonomous decision makers regarding the curriculum they use. Teachers who encounter curricula in many forms, which were discussed in the previous chapter, may have all sorts of questions about the
curriculum materials they use. It was presumed that these questions reveal some of teachers' own concerns about curriculum.

In order to find out what questions concerned teachers, a special instrument was developed consisting of forty questions about curriculum materials and was designated as Curriculum Characteristics Inventory (CCI). Curriculum characteristics reflected in this instrument represent several broad categories which are assumed to play a major role in curriculum development, namely, subject matter, students, and teachers. Items about the nature of the subject matter, as reflected in the materials, the anticipated adaptations to student characteristics, and the role expectations for teachers, were therefore included in the questionnaire. The following are some examples of items related to these categories:

In the "subject matter" category:

• Are principles and concepts of the discipline emphasized in the materials?
• Do the curriculum materials provide learners with a broad knowledge of subject matter?

In the "student" category:

• Can the curriculum materials be adapted to students of different ability levels?
• Is the level of the target student population specified?

In the "teacher" category:

• Do the curriculum materials provide the teacher with alternatives for choice?
• Does the teacher's guide explain the considerations of the curriculum developers?

Seventy secondary school biology teachers and eighty-five teachers of other subject matter areas responded to the Curriculum Characteristics Inventory (CCI) questionnaire, in which items were put in the form of questions that could be addressed to curriculum materials. Two modes of responses were requested: (1) rating of each item in the questionnaire, each question about curriculum materials, on a 6-point scale in which 1 = not important and 6 = very important, and (2) ranking of the five most important and five least important items.

Teachers showed the highest level of concern for the "subject matter" aspect of curriculum materials. On the other hand, questions related to the role of the teachers were conceived as least important. The high priority all teachers accord to the "subject matter" category is consistent with findings of studies dealing with teacher planning showing that teachers spend a large proportion of their planning on content decisions (Taylor 1970; Clark and Yinger 1977). On the other hand, it seems that teachers are not very interested in questions related to the "teacher" aspect of the curriculum. One possible explanation for these findings is that teachers expect curriculum materials to focus on the content of teaching and on considerations related to students, and they accept this as a legitimate and defensible orientation. Teachers may not expect curriculum materials to deal with the mode of interaction between themselves and the materials. One may conclude that teachers do not give priority to questions about "teachers" because they tend to adopt the role of independent decision maker. In that case, since teachers will automatically make decisions they consider appropriate to the circumstances of their classroom, it is of no great consequence to them whether the curriculum materials provide alternative options, nor does the teacher guide seem very important.

The ranking order of specific items reveals an interesting picture. In the "subject matter" category the highest ranking goes to "emphasis on principles and concepts of the discipline" and the lowest to "prerequisite knowledge in other disciplines." This result may be a reflection of teachers' acceptance of the educational approach that argues for the importance of knowledge of principles. It seems that teachers in this study tend to disregard the previous learning experiences of their students and take upon themselves full responsibility for whatever learning occurs in their classes. In the category of "student," the highest ranking was assigned to the "adaptability of curriculum materials to students of different ability levels," and the lowest to the "specification of the target population." The question of whether the materials are potentially adaptable to a range of ability levels seems to be more important to teachers than whether the developers have designed the materials with a specific target population in mind. It seems that teachers are aware of their intimate knowledge of classroom realities and students' needs and are therefore interested in flexible curriculum materials which may be easily changed and modified. The lowest ranking assigned to the "specification of detailed objectives" is congruent with similar findings already mentioned, which indicate that teachers think in terms of content and students' activities rather than in terms of objectives. This finding supports Schwab's (1983) claim that "curriculum is not an endless collection of objectives" (p. 240). Curriculum is the lived-in teaching-learning experience of teachers and students, and is thus perceived by teachers. In the "teacher" category the highest ranking was assigned to "teachers autonomy to choose and initiate teaching strategies." This finding supports the interpretation that the low position assigned to the category of "teacher" reflects teachers' self-confidence in their ability to use the material appropriately without lockstep directions from curriculum developers.

The emerging image that teachers seem to have regarding their own role in curriculum issues has to be viewed in the context of the conflicting messages that teachers may receive from the educational establishment. On the one hand, teachers may be called upon to introduce curricular innovations as faithfully as possible. On the other hand, teachers may be aware of growing expectations to act as autonomous professionals and to be actively involved in the process of curriculum implementation as adaptors and modifiers of existing materials (Berman and McLaughlin 1977; Connelly and Ben-Peretz 1980). There seems to be a growing awareness that active involvement of teachers in the molding of curriculum materials according to their specific situation is crucial for the successful introduction of innovations into the educational system. This awareness is apparently shared by teachers.

IMPLICATIONS FOR TEACHERS' CONCERNS ABOUT CURRICULUM MATERIALS

Responses of teachers to the Curriculum Characteristics Inventory (CCI) questionnaire reveal several of their concerns about curriculum materials. Teachers are apparently concerned *about the nature of the content presented in the materials*. They seem to be aware of the need to emphasize principles and basic concepts, and they ask themselves if the materials they use follow this approach. In a sense, the teachers who participated in this study seem to have internalized the view that the best way to deal with the teaching of any subject matter area is to provide students with general principles. In other words, teachers accepted the "structure of knowledge" curricular approach.[4] It may be that teachers' emphasis on principles and concepts is in itself the result of having used innovative curriculum materials which reflected this approach.

It is interesting to note the congruency of this finding with

Goodlad's (1984) conclusion that teachers "agreed, generally, on the importance of basic skills and subject matter and on increasing students' store of information about the various fields of knowledge" (p. 174). Teachers' concerns about issues of content seem to be well established.

Another major concern of teachers relates to the *adaptability of materials to divergent student needs*. Many classes are heterogeneous, and teachers may find themselves in a position of having to deal simultaneously with several levels of interest, ability, and knowledge. Curriculum materials which are rich in opportunities for adaptation to different student needs assist teachers in their task. Butt et al. (1986) defined the key issue as "the degree to which the curriculum is adequate, in and of itself, and the degree to which presciption, external testing and specific subject matter is perceived to allow for flexible adaptation, in terms of both content and pedagogy, to meet pupils' needs and interests, as well as the teacher's style and beliefs" (p. 316). We have already discussed the finding that teachers were not overly concerned whether the materials treat teachers as "choice makers," probably because teachers naturally assume this to be their role and function in curriculum implementation.

Lortie (1975) found similar concerns that teachers have regarding the curriculum materials they use. Teachers are concerned about the quality of textbooks and want better and more up-to-date books. According to Lortie, teachers desire better facilities and more flexible curricula which increase student options.

What are the main concerns you have about your curriculum? Are you personally involved in decisions about the adoption of curriculum materials, and if so, how do your concerns shape your decisions? You may be interested in discussing these issues with your colleagues.

CURRICULUM COVERAGE

A persistent theme of teachers' curricular concerns seems to be whether they should aim at maximum coverage of materials or at in-depth teaching of certain selected issues. Teachers are enormously sensitive to the coverage of curriculum content that will be tested. They adapt their teaching in order to prepare their students for forthcoming examinations (Ben-Peretz 1980b). There is evidence for the impact that external examinations have on the coverage of curriculum items. Connelly et al. (1978) found that the curriculum implemented by biology teachers and the textbooks they use are congruent with the demands of the examination and cover the prescribed biological principles and specific knowledge units. Similar findings are reported by Tamir and Glassman (1971), who investigated the impact of the practical examination in biology on the instructional choices of teachers.

Concern for "coverage" is complicated even further because even attempts to provide students with detailed information about any subject is apt to yield very meagre results. An interesting example of this phenomenon may be found in the teaching of the Holocaust in Israel. In 1980 the teaching of this topic became obligatory for the twelfth (last) grade of high school. A curriculum of thirty hours was developed, trying to "cover" the most essential facts. Textbooks were written, and today two of the many in existence are used in most high schools.[5] Those thirty hours and the "coverage" of a textbook do not yield the desired outcomes. Students who took an elective course on the Holocaust at the school of education at the University of Haifa did not know the essential, basic facts, even though all of them had matriculated after 1980, and all of them had a strong motivation to choose this course (M. Lifmann, personal communication).

One of the issues of this book is the delicate balancing between faithful coverage of the curriculum and individual choices that may lead to flexible adaptation of the materials and to more meaningful learning experiences.

LACK OF CURRICULAR KNOWLEDGE

Many teachers seem to share an additional crucial concern: a lack of knowledge about, and opportunities to engage in, curriculum development. This lack of curricular knowledge may limit teachers' abilities to use existing materials creatively and flexibly. Teachers' education programs may stress a stance which rejects reliance on externally prepared curriculum materials. Loewenberg-Ball and Feiman-Nemser (1988) point out that all the student-teachers who participated in their study of preservice teacher education developed the impression that if they want to be good teachers they should avoid following textbooks and teachers' guides, that "it all has to come from you" (p. 414). The researchers argue that this stance poses a crucial dilemma. Although externally prepared curricula do not necessarily address the specific needs of students and teachers alike, student-teachers lack knowledge and experience for developing their own curriculum, and they are fully aware of this situation.

It seems that relatively little emphasis is put on teacher preparation for curriculum planning. Silberstein (1982) found that the majority of teachers in colleges of teacher education claimed that they devoted less than five periods to the topic of preparing student-teachers for their task as curriculum implementors and potential curriculum developers. Although lesson planning is generally discussed and practiced, little attention is given to the in-depth learning of curricular processes.

It would seem that practicing teachers are hardly in a better position. Goodlad (1984) argues that one of the shortcomings of the curriculum reform movement was that it did not create links to teacher education programs. Consequently, teachers lack necessary curricular knowledge. Rudduck (1987) claims that "opportunities for extending the curriculum literacy of teachers have been lost" (p. 82).

Tilemma and De Jong (1986), studying teachers' task perception and professional competencies in the Netherlands, found that about 36 percent of principals and teachers, and about 67 percent of "change agents," claim that they need further education in curriculum development.[6] Professionalizing is deemed necessary by teachers in areas of innovation which are directly related to their regular teaching repertoire. These findings indicate a need for dealing seriously with curricular issues in teacher education programs and in staff development. We shall return to this issue in Chapter 7.

THE ROLE OF TEACHERS FROM THE PERSPECTIVE OF CURRICULUM DEVELOPERS

It is interesting to note that the apparent ambiguity surrounding teachers' roles regarding the curriculum may be shared by curriculum developers. Analysis of six teacher guides in various subject matter areas (Silberstein and Ben-Peretz 1987) showed that only in three of the guides were teachers treated as autonomous implementors. These teacher guides informed teachers about the reasons behind the curricular decisions made by the developers. Teachers were expected, even advised, to introduce changes into the materials. They were regarded as experts, both in the specific subject matter area and in the domain of instructional strategies. In other teachers' guides very little anticipation of teachers' involvement in adaptation and change was found.

The lack of information about choices made by curriculum developers or writers of textbooks makes it difficult for teachers to reach defensible decisions regarding choices and changes in the curriculum. For instance, curriculum developers may decide to introduce the following passage into an eighth grade biology textbook:

> Many researchers in this country invest a great deal of effort in the exploration of possible savings in the amount of water needed for watering a variety of cultivated plants. Citrus production, one of the important export lines, is a target of these efforts. In the year 1970–1971 about 336 million cubic metres of water were consumed by citrus groves. (CM—"The Plant and Its Environment," 1974, p. 13)

The developers may believe that this passage would be perceived by students as relevant and motivating because of students' everyday experiences related to a perennial shortage of water supply. Teachers who are unaware of the developers' reasoning may be inclined to think that the specific content included in this passage is inherently important. They may even ask their students to memorize the figures supplied in the text. Sharing with teachers the grounds for choosing specific content and style of curriculum materials may provide the necessary basis for teachers' choices and adaptations.

Rudduck (1987) comments that, instead of trying to provide practitioners with curriculum literacy, "curriculum developers have often chosen to act like 'columnists and commentators' who are protectively selective in their disclosures of the logic of the situations they report" (p. 82). What can be done to change this situation? Improving systems of staff development, creating opportunities for sharing problems, commenting on each others' performance, and collaborating in planning of curriculum implementation could serve to improve the quality of teaching. Different processes which may support teachers' collaboration will be dealt with further on.

CONCLUDING COMMENTS

In their daily work teachers encounter curriculum materials in a variety of forms. Often they are called upon to implement these materials, and sometimes they create their own school-based curriculum.

Teachers have varied concerns about curriculum materials and are sometimes overwhelmed by their curricular tasks. One of the principal dilemmas of teachers is the dilemma of teacher autonomy, as reflected in the role teachers are expected to play regarding the curriculum. Though teachers tend to see themselves in control of what they teach and how they teach (Goodlad 1984), there exists an ambiguity about their curricular roles. Are teachers expected to be faithful implementors of curriculum materials developed externally, or are they to act as adaptors of external curricula and creators of school-based curriculum? Do schools offer appropriate conditions for either role? Are teachers prepared for autonomous curriculum planning? Is professional teacher autonomy a myth and a slogan only, hardly realized in the many schools in which teachers tend to follow their textbooks page after page? And yet, in planning their courses and their daily lessons, teachers interpret the various forms of curriculum materials and transform the written documents into a "curriculum in use," planning concrete learning experiences. Teachers know their students and are familiar with the complexities of their classrooms. Teachers may also have their own purposes and educational priorities. These goal priorities might not necessarily coincide with the set of priorities of the curriculum developers. Instead of trying in vain to make curricula "teacher-proof," it might be better to provide teachers with "curricular possibilities" as a basis for choice and action. It should also be borne in mind that curriculum developers themselves may view their prepared materials more as sources for teacher planning than as rigid frameworks to be imposed on schools. Interpretations of curriculum materials, whether these are general guidelines or elaborated instructional materials, create the conditions of learning in the classroom and shape the process of learning as experienced by students. Both the processes and the products of learning are determined, to a large extent, by the teacher's expertise in interpreting curriculum materials.

In the following chapters a framework for enhancing teacher

expertise in curriculum interpretation will be presented and elaborated.

RECOMMENDED ADDITIONAL READINGS

You may wish to read more about teachers and their views about their daily tasks. An excellent book dealing with these issues is Dan Lortie's *Schoolteacher: A Sociological Study* (1975): Chicago, University of Chicago Press.

A book about teacher thinking which captures some of teachers' concerns is *Teacher Thinking: A New Perspective on Persisting Problems in Education* (1984): R. Halkes and J. K. Olson (eds.), Lisse, Swets and Zeitlinger.

Special attention to the relationship between teachers and the curriculum is found in "Teachers and curriculum materials: Who is driving whom?" by A. Reynolds et al. (1988): *Curriculum Perspectives* 8, 1:22–29.

The following paper discusses curriculum decisions by teachers: MacDonald, R. A., and Leithwood, K. A. (1982): "Toward an explanation of influences on teachers' curriculum decisions," in K. A. Leithwood (ed.), *Studies in Curriculum Decision Making*, Symposium Series 13, Toronto, OISE Press.

4

The Concept of Curriculum Potential

"There is beauty in everything, but
not everyone is capable of seeing it"

Confucius, 551–478 B.C.

Up to this point we have discussed different ways in which teachers may become involved in curriculum endeavors, and their personal concerns relating to this involvement were considered. Different forms of curriculum that teachers may encounter in their daily work were presented. Now we turn to a discussion of the nature of curriculum materials. The basic approach adopted here is that curriculum materials constitute an expression of educational potential, of intended, as well as unintended, curricular uses which may be disclosed through deliberate interpretation efforts (Ben-Peretz 1975).[7] This chapter will elaborate on the notion of curriculum potential and its implications for educational practice.

CURRICULUM MATERIALS AS EMBODIMENTS OF POTENTIAL

Although curriculum materials are often perceived as the expression of their developers' intentions, Schwab (1973) warns us that these intentions convey the values of the developers only imperfectly and merely suggest ways of constructing teaching activities. Actual classroom experiences of the curriculum might serve to reduce the ambiguity of the stated intentions as well as to modify them. Implementation of ideas and activities which are proposed in the curriculum turns these into concrete experiences. These experiences may correspond to the perceived intentions of the developers, but they may also serve different ends.

Let us look at a documented example of such a case. Hamilton (1975) described and analyzed the implementation of curriculum innovations in science in two Scottish schools. The most significant features of this curricular innovation were (1) its integration

45

of physics, chemistry, and biology; (2) the intention that one teacher should teach all science lessons; (3) its dependence on "guided discovery methods" (engagement of students in active investigations guided by the textbook and by their teachers); and (4) its reliance on multiple choice examinations for testing whether the stated objectives had been achieved. The curriculum materials include a general discussion of the course, a series of instructional recommendations, an outline of the content, 210 specific educational objectives, and sets of worksheets which were intended to support "learning by discovery." In his study Hamilton observed science lessons in two different schools. In one of these he found that the implementation of the course did not match the picture of integrated science presented by the curriculum documents.

Hamilton presented several examples of this state of affairs, for instance: "Instead of support materials the worksheets had become *the* syllabus; and as teacher demonstrations were often substituted for pupil practical work, class teaching had become the dominant activity" (p. 187). He noted that the style of teaching depended on available time and on other contextual features: "Inclement weather. Teacher dictating names of trees rather than allowing children out into the school grounds to find out for themselves—as was the original intention. Also wants to get finished and have section 2 tests before half-term" (p. 197). In this example we can see how different intentions of the curriculum developers seem to result in certain contradictions in practice. Open-ended learning by discovery clashed with the prescription of repeated testing. Tests were deployed in order to grade pupils rather than to serve as diagnostic tools. According to Hamilton, some of the students were aware of the discriminatory function of tests and voiced their conviction that the main reason for science tests was to stream students into learning groups. Hamilton goes on to state that "needless to say, a range of unintended effects flowed from the teachers' misinterpretation" (p. 200). For example, the setting of tests simultaneously in different classes caused a ranking of classes according to their achievements, an effect not implied by the curriculum papers. Hamilton argues that "however explicitly expressed in curriculum papers or teacher guides, aims and objectives require reinterpretation in practice" (pp. 190–191). The curriculum implementation case documented by Hamilton is one example of modification, even distortion, of developers' intentions.

Another example illuminates modification of the intentions of curriculum developers in order to accommodate perceived student needs (Ben-Peretz 1975). A set of reflection cards was developed as part of a new math program for elementary schools. The intention of the developers was to teach invariants of reflections as an intuitive preparation for the learning of geometry and functions. The recommended teaching strategy was individual student work, each child learning and testing his or her own progress independently, with little intervention by teachers. The nonverbal curriculum material did not include any explanatory text. The cards showed abstract figures which were chosen by the developers so as not to distract learners from their tasks. Trial implementation of the materials revealed possible uses and learning outcomes not intended by developers. Although the materials were structured in such a way that teachers' intervention in the learning process became superfluous, some teachers did take on an active role in teaching. Some told stories to promote student understanding; others encouraged children to name the figures they produced with the reflection cards and to express their perceptions in writing or painting. Thus the reflection cards became stimuli for creative activities. Experience with the reflection cards showed that, although intended for the development of mathematical concepts, they could also be used in other subject matter areas, such as language and art.

Both cases discussed so far are examples of curriculum interpretation by teachers, who use the materials in ways which go beyond the explicit intentions of their developers. The integrated science case may be viewed as representing misinterpretations of the curriculum that lead to its distortion and failure. The new math case may be perceived as representing teacher interpretations of materials which reveal curriculum potential, leading to pedagogical enrichment. Both cases confirm Schwab's (1973) notion that actual classroom experiences might modify the intentions of developers because of reinterpretations carried out by teachers using the curriculum materials.

It is important to note that the notion of 'curriculum potential' implies two interacting elements. One concerns the nature of the materials: more complex and comprehensive materials may yield a richer array of possible uses. On the other hand, it may be possible to use rather limited and standard materials and to create exciting and motivating experiences. The "reading" of curriculum potential depends not only on the inherent qualities of the materials, but also, to a large extent, on teachers' interpretive abilities and on their professional imagination. How to develop these abilities is the central theme of the following chapters.

Empirical evidence for the phenomenon of curriculum interpretation by teachers, and for the reality of curriculum potential, is supported by a conceptual issue raised by Meyer (1972). Meyer pointed to a problem of deduction which constitutes a major difficulty in the classic model of curriculum development. It is sometimes assumed that developers start with the specification of objectives which guide the choice of learning content and instructional activities. Yet the movement from goals to activities cannot be demonstrated to be a logical outcome of a series of deductions starting with general goals, moving to specific objectives, and terminating in decisions about content and didactic procedures. Various curricular decisions may legitimately result from one projected goal, but different goals may be served by one curricular decision. Two imagined situations will serve to exemplify this point.

Curriculum developers who intend to promote a sense of responsibility toward the environment might decide to focus on the uniqueness of human beings and stress their consequent obligations to the conservation of other organisms and the ecosystem. On the other hand, developers with the same intentions and goals might decide to stress the common characteristics of human beings and other living organisms, hoping to minimize self-centeredness. This approach, too, may be seen as promoting a heightened sense of obligation toward the environment. In these instances the same intentions and goals lead to the development of different kinds of curriculum materials, different content, and different teaching strategies.

Another possible case exemplifies a situation in which one unit, the product of one curricular decision, may serve different educational goals. Developers dealing with the theory of evolution might decide to create a curriculum unit about the famous Scopes trial, in which the teaching of evolutionary theory was challenged. Various objectives, such as providing students with insights into the intricate relationships between science and society, might be considered by the developers. The same unit might also be used in a social science program in order to give students an insight into the judiciary apparatus of the United States, or in a drama program through reenactment of the trial in the classroom. Thus, the same curriculum unit may be used in the service of different educational goals.

These speculative curricular situations suggest that it is inappropriate to view any set of curriculum materials purely as an embodiment of writers' intentions. Curriculum materials are more complex and richer in educational potential than can be expressed in any list of preconceived goals or objectives, whether general or specific. If we look upon curriculum materials as the end product of a creative development process, then any single interpretation is bound to yield only a partial picture of the manifold aspects of the educational possibilities that these materials represent.

Tyler (1949) was fully aware that many particular experiences can be used to obtain the same objective and that the same experiences may serve several objectives. Atkins (1970) demonstrates vividly how many possible objectives may ensue from one simple learning activity, such as blowing against a mealworm through a straw. Although the planner of this activity may have intended it to promote learning about mealworm behavior, it may serve many more "objectives," among them learning about one's ability to manipulate the environment, possible uses of a plastic straw, and others too numerous to mention. This is another example of the "deduction problem."

CURRICULUM POTENTIAL AND UNINTENDED LEARNING OUTCOMES

At this point it is important to differentiate between the well-known phenomenon of "unintended outcomes" of instruction (also termed "incidental learning"), on the one hand, and the reinterpretation of curriculum materials by teachers leading to classroom uses beyond the scope of developers' intentions, on the other hand. Unintended outcomes are almost inevitable consequences of all teaching acts in any circumstances. For instance, growing doubts about one's own ability to understand mathematics is but one example of the unintended consequences of some modes of teaching math. Jackson (1986) discusses the moral and transformative dimensions of teachers' work which may cause qualitative changes in the person being taught. Jackson argues that the teachers may, indeed, "modify character, instil values, shape attitudes, generate new interests, and succeed in 'transforming', profoundly and enduringly, at least some of the students in their charge" (p. 123). The changes in students that are described by Jackson may be considered to be in the realm of unintended outcomes. There are, according to Jackson, no formulas or instructions which may serve as guides for teachers who would like to have a transformative impact on their students. There are, however, according to Jackson, certain characteristic "modes of operation," like personal modeling, which may influence one's students.

The disclosing of curriculum potential is perceived differently; it is not incidental but an outcome of skillful and deliberate teacher interpretation of curriculum materials. Deliberate planning of specific experiences follows this interpretation, sometimes resulting in uses that may be considered unacceptable by curriculum developers. In spite of this possibility, it is contended that curriculum interpretation by teachers, along with the discovery of varied forms of curriculum potential, is extremely important and may lead to flexible and adaptive uses of curriculum materials.

CURRICULUM POTENTIAL AND THE HIDDEN CURRICULUM

How is the notion of 'curriculum potential' related to the notion of the 'hidden curriculum'? Is the discovery of curriculum potential to be equated with the uncovering of the hidden curriculum?

According to one definition by Martin (1976), "a hidden curriculum consists of some of the outcomes or by-products of schools or of nonschool settings, particularly those states which are learned yet are not openly intended" (p. 137). Gordon (1988) defines the hidden curriculum as "the unintended messages transmitted by the physical and social structure of the school, and by the teaching process itself" (p. 425). The messages transmitted by the hidden curriculum and the unintended learning that takes place are generally considered to be in the domain of values, attitudes, and beliefs. These unintended learning experiences are part of the curriculum in use, enacted in live and concrete classroom.

The definitions mentioned above stress the "unintendedness" and implicitness of the hidden curriculum, as opposed to the intentional and manifold nature of the explicit curriculum which is stated openly by developers and policymakers. Martin (1976) amends her definition by stating that "a hidden curriculum consists of those learning states of a setting which are either unintended or intended but not openly acknowledged to the learners in the setting" (p. 144). Still, even in this definition the intentions are not stated openly, and are unknown to learners.

Curriculum potential is conceived as implicitly embedded in curriculum; in this sense it is similar to the hidden curriculum. Yet, crucial distinctions have to be made. Martin (1976) claims "that any aspect of an educational setting can have learning states which are not openly intended" (p. 141). In this sense, hidden curricula are an inseparable, almost natural, component of all educational situations. The realization of curriculum potential, on the other hand, is not a natural component of classroom situations. Teachers have to be actively and intentionally involved in uncovering multiple uses of curriculum materials in their setting. Moreover, these uses and their anticipated outcomes usually become part of the manifest and openly stated curriculum for the students. The concept of 'curriculum potential' and the concept of the 'hidden curriculum' share the aspect of being concealed, implicit in the curriculum. In both cases acts of deliberate uncovering are necessary before educators become aware of their existence. Yet, whereas the hidden curriculum is conceived mainly in its negative affective aspects, curriculum potential is perceived as a highly positive facet of curriculum, strongly related to cognitive aspects of the materials. Still, these concepts are linked, and it may be possible for teachers to use their awareness of the hidden curriculum as a starting point for developing curriculum potential.[8]

CURRICULUM POTENTIAL AND THE NULL CURRICULUM

Schools may be perceived as teaching three curricula: the explicit, the implicit (the hidden), and the null (Eisner 1979). We have discussed the explicit and implicit curricula and turn now to the notion of the "null" curriculum.

The *null curriculum* refers to areas of subject matter, intellectual processes, and values which are left out of the constructed curriculum. No set of curriculum materials can contain everything. Decisions have to be made about those components which are left out. For instance, a set of curriculum materials in biology may omit the concept of evolution. This omission may be intentional and related to the ideological convictions of the developers. Not all omissions are necessarily intentional, resulting from developers' careful consideration of alternatives. Sometimes lacunas in the curriculum are caused by lack of developers' knowledge in a field. For instance, curriculum developers in science may omit all references to the history and philosophy of science because they are unfamiliar with these topics. Whether intentional or unintentional, the null curriculum plays a significant role in education because it determines to a large extent the knowledge base of learners, of the future members of society. The notion of the null curriculum is extremely important in relation to the concept of curriculum potential (Connelly and Clandinin 1988). Missing elements of a curriculum, once identified by teachers, may become the starting point for teacher involvement in the creation of complementary curricular elements. For instance, a science teacher who is aware of the lack of historical and personal information about scientists in the curriculum materials may decide to include these excluded topics in his or her teaching. Additional materials may be created and linked to the existing curriculum text.

It is important to remember that the notion of curriculum potential is dependent on the interaction between teachers and materials. Materials offer starting points, and teachers use their curricular insights, their pedagogical knowledge, and their professional imagination to develop their own curricular ideas on the basis of existing materials. The scope, variety, and richness of the curriculum potential embodied in materials is determined by the wealth of their content and the flexibility or rigidity of their structure. "Good curriculum materials have many different potentials for different people in different circumstances. As teachers, we must realize this potential" (Connelly and Clandinin 1988, p. 152). The spectrum of ideas about potential uses of curriculum materials that teachers may generate is dependent on their knowledge of subject matter, their past teaching experiences, their feeling for and understanding of classroom reality, their interpretative skills, and their openness to new ideas. Teaching experiences such as unusual student questions, as well as particular classroom conditions, for instance, the lack of equipment, may lead to innovative uses of materials based on their perceived potential.

Until now we have discussed curricular concepts: curriculum potential, unintended learning outcomes, and the hidden and the null curriculum. You may find it useful now to think about your own teaching and the curriculum materials you use. Imagine what you might do in your classroom by going beyond the explicit intentions of the materials. How would you enrich your teaching through different uses of the text? Try to make a list of topics and activities which could have been included in your text but were excluded. What kinds of intellectual processes could be brought into play? What values and attitudes could be probed? Try to note instances in your practice in which you used your materials differently and creatively. How could you involve your own students in your curricular deliberations? You may wish to share with your colleagues reflections about curriculum potential.

EXAMPLES OF CURRICULUM POTENTIAL

We turn now to some concrete examples of uses of curriculum potential in different educational situations. One example relates to the curriculum potential of role-playing exercises in science and technology (CM—CREST 1986). The main objective of the role-playing situation is to enable students to explain and discuss the social, political, and economic factors that influence decisions on issues of science and technology. The way in which the unit is set out is one of inquiry. The students are given background information and carry out their own investigations. Then they gather in a "council meeting" to defend their viewpoints, and a course of action is chosen by the simulated governing body (city, state). The structure of the unit does not give the students freedom to incorporate their own ideas into the role-playing because the personality descriptions in the role cards cover everything from marital status to beliefs held by the role representatives. The students are asked to reenact a conflict in U.S. history. They are being put through the paces of problem solving, and the developers hope that students will adopt this approach to problem solving in future instances of confrontations with problem situations.

Let us listen to a teacher who participated in a curriculum meeting discussing her use of this curriculum unit (personal communication):

> We immediately deviated from the time line by using local resources to supplement the first discussion. Also we paid little attention to the designation of role cards (male or female, to match the role names). We let students investigate the topic and then had minicouncil meetings in which students debated informally. There was no final council decision but rather a discussion of the manner in which

various factors affect decision making and the difficulty involved in making such decisions. Each character would perceive a wide range of possible decisions. Many students introduced modifications in their role cards and incorporated factors which they felt were relevant and important. They discussed how the role may reflect their possible orientation to the issue and the decisions that they may some day have to make as community members. In the debriefing session, we did not follow the questions given in the unit.

The teacher explained how her previous experiences shaped her interpretation of the unit.

In retrospect, other factors which probably affected our orientation to the CREST program were two option units that we had jointly offered in previous terms. We did a novel study of *Brave New World* by Aldous Huxley, on how technology can change society. We also offered an option on the novels *The Crystallides*, by John Wyndham, and *A Canticle for Leibowitz*, by Walter M. Miller, Jr. These novels look at societal structure after a nuclear holocaust. With this in mind, we analyzed the novels and had the students create their own societies at various stages after a holocaust. They chose the initial survivors (after we outlined numbers in terms of population distribution in relation to working class, elite, etc.), and chose political, economic and religious orientations of their societies. These previous encounters with Science-Technology-Society-related topics gave me the confidence to deviate from the material and ignore the specified objectives outlined by the CREST program. I feel that we made modifications which were reflective of *our* aims for the unit, to allow students to see the social side of science-related technology. [emphasis added]

This teacher described her process of deriving the educational potential of a structured curriculum unit. Her intepretation of the unit is modified by previous experiences in teaching literature and by her own attitudes and beliefs. For instance, the teacher was upset by the designation of functions in the societal structure which were implicit in the assigned role description. She stated, for instance, that "the cards with male names tend to be people of higher education and in powerful positions." Her personal interpretation of the materials led her to change some of the learning activities. Her planning was influenced by former experiences with studies of relevant novels. This is an interesting example of the "cross-fertilization" between subject matter areas in the process of teacher planning based on the perceived potential of materials.

Another example of curriculum potential was chosen from an analysis of four cases of social studies teaching (Gudmunsdottir 1988). One of these cases is about an experienced teacher of history who teaches American history to a general-track class. The formal curriculum covers the period from the discovery of America by Columbus to the present day. The textbook is divided into chronological periods. Not all the periods treated by the teacher correspond to the textbook. This teacher has developed his own four "stories" that he communicates through the curriculum: "The Growth of Opportunities, the Age of Discoveries, Clash of Cultures and Transformation of Cultures and Institutions—Each story highlights different topics in the curriculum, connecting them to similar ideas previously covered" (Gudmunsdottir 1988, p. 6). This teacher's interpretation of his curriculum is based on his thorough subject matter knowledge and his ability to maintain complex stories through a whole school year. According to Gudmunsdottir:

> Curriculum stories help teachers manage complex ideas and make them accessible for students. For the stories to function effectively they need a central idea that is strong enough to shape the events that contribute to the development of the plot. The experienced teachers have such stories. The curriculum stories are central to their pedagogical content knowledge. (Gudmunsdottir 1988, p. 9)

Creation of one's own "curriculum stories" is one of the ways in which teachers realize the potential of curriculum materials. There is a strong link between the ability to discern curriculum potential and pedagogical content knowledge. Pedagogical content knowledge was defined by Shulman (1987) as the professional blending of content and pedagogy which enables teachers to organize and adapt teaching topics to diverse student populations. Pedagogical content knowledge develops over years of teaching experience.[9] Teachers' use of curriculum potential is based on their pedagogical content knowledge. Each case of realized potential, such as "curriculum stories," becomes, in turn, part of the professional knowledge base of teachers.

You may try to analyze one of your own cases of curriculum change and adaptation, realizing some of the educational potential of the materials. Ask yourself how your actions were related to your previous teaching experiences. Could you describe your own pedagogical content knowledge in relation to this case?

TEACHERS AS USER-DEVELOPERS

In the cases presented here, teachers adopt the role of independent interpretors of curriculum materials who seek new ways of handling the materials and discover educational possibilities not foreseen by the developers. This role is congruent with Connelly's approach to teachers as "user-developers" (Connelly 1972). According to Connelly, teachers fulfill a development role in the curriculum enterprise, even when implementing externally prepared curricula. This role implies choices and modifications planned by teachers who try to adapt curriculum materials to specific and changing classroom situations. Developers and teachers may best be seen as supporting each other in curriculum development by virtue of their different, but obviously related, roles. This relationship, which decisively shifts the teacher's role from faithful implementor to decision maker and independent developer, is described as follows:

> The strength and major contribution of a developer are that he works with and can translate involved ideas into a form useful for teachers and students. However, the developer cannot imagine, let alone account for, the full range of teaching situations that arise. It is here that the teacher's experience and wisdom enter into curriculum planning in a way that cannot adequately be replaced. The characteristics and needs of the actual classroom situation are the first and final factors determining what should be done in that classroom. The teacher is inescapably the arbiter between the demands of curriculum materials and of the instructional situation. Only rarely will arbitration lead to a settlement exclusively favouring the developers' intentions. (Connelly 1972, p. 164)

The role of autonomous interpretors of curriculum materials and as partners in development is but one of the possible roles teachers may be assumed to play in the process of curriculum implementation. The different roles are presented diagramatically in Figure 1. Three images of the possible role of teachers emerge:

(a) Teachers may be treated as transmitters of curricular ideas through "teacher-proof" materials. A variety of such materials were designed to ensure the accurate realization of developers' curricular ideas in the classrooms. Teachers, especially inexperienced teachers, may view any set of materials as "teacher-proof," may feel limited in their freedom to consider change, and may doubt the legitimacy of adapation.

(b) Another view recognizes the considerable influence teachers have on the implementation of curricular ideas. This view may lead to the attempt to "convert" teachers to the ideas and practices embodied in curriculum materials by way of workshops and other training activities.

(c) A third approach to the role of teachers assumes teachers to be full partners in the process of curriculum development as "user-developers" (Connelly 1972). Teachers are expected to adapt and mold curriculum materials to their own purposes and to the requirements of their specific educational situations. According to this view, there is no one predetermined set of goals for a set of curriculum materials, but rather an array of possible goals depending on how the teacher interprets and uses the potential embodied in curriculum materials (Ben-Peretz 1975).

This third approach is the approach advocated in this book.

HOW TO REVEAL CURRICULUM POTENTIAL?

The examples of teachers who found new ways to use curriculum materials clarify an important point. Teachers rely on their personal experiences, on their practical knowledge, and on pedagogical content knowledge in their attempts to create their own versions of curricular ideas. Jackson (1986) offers interesting insights into the nature of teachers' expertise. He states that "expert teach-

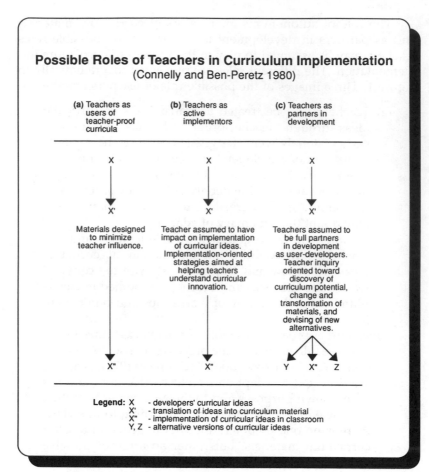

Possible Roles of Teachers in Curriculum Implementation
(Connelly and Ben-Peretz 1980)

(a) Teachers as users of teacher-proof curricula

(b) Teachers as active implementors

(c) Teachers as partners in development

X → X'

X → X'

X → X'

Materials designed to minimize teacher influence.

Teacher assumed to have impact on implementation of curricular ideas. Implementation-oriented strategies aimed at helping teachers understand curricular innovation.

Teachers assumed to be full partners in development as user-developers. Teacher inquiry oriented toward discovery of curriculum potential, change and transformation of materials, and devising of new alternatives.

X"

X"

Y X" Z

Legend: X   - developers' curricular ideas
X' - translation of ideas into curriculum material
X" - implementation of curricular ideas in classroom
Y, Z - alternative versions of curricular ideas

ers 'see more' than do nonexperts" (p. 87). Three specific features are suggested by Jackson as characterizing experts in teaching:

1. Experts are expected to have a differentiated perception of the objects of their expertise.
2. Experts are able to be quicker in their perceptions.
3. Experts would be expected to to see possibilities where others see none.

Classrooms and teaching situations consist of manifold possible objects of teachers' expertise. Teachers may be experts in knowing students and in understanding the complexities of the social and ecological environment of schools. In order to disclose the rich educational potential embodied in curriculum materials, teachers have to be experts in curriculum interpretations. Such expertise will allow them to "see more," in a more differentiated and quicker way. Such expertise will enable them to become user-developers and see possibilities which are beyond the intentions of curriculum developers.

Before turning to modes and instruments of curriculum interpretation, let us try to summarize briefly some of the characteristics of the curriculum development process as carried out by external developers, in comparison with the characteristics of development carried out by teachers as user-developers. Let us call the process of external curriculum development "the first level of curriculum interpretation." This is the transformation of scholarly subject matter knowledge into curriculum materials. Transformation of curriculum materials into learning experiences is carried out by teachers at the "second level of curriculum interpretation" (Ben-Peretz and Silberstein 1982).

Some elements are common to the two levels of interpretation:

a. The external developers and the teachers who function as user-developers reach decisions about three main issues: content, instructional strategies, and the context of teaching.
b. Many of the considerations guiding the decisions of external developers and user-developers originate in their personal knowledge, as shaped by previous experiences, and in their belief systems.

The characteristics of each level of interpretation may be summed up as follows:

First level of interpretation	Second level of interpretation
1. The development process is *convergent* in the sense that it ends in the creation of curriculum materials defined by certain predetermined characteristics, and yet rich in educational potential beyond developers' intentions.	The process of teacher planning is *divergent* and leads to different and individual teaching-learning settings of different teachers and of the same teacher in varying circumstances.
2. The external developers are largely concerned with the definition and clarification of content elements and possible educational messages to be conveyed to the students.	Teachers may be less concerned with the definition and clarification of possible additional content elements. They select from existing content, deciding on which elements to focus and how to interpret and restructure it for teaching.
3. External developers tend to propose a relatively limited variety of instructional strategies.	Teachers are aware of the importance of instructional strategies and the need to adapt them to their particular educational circumstances. They initiate new strategies beyond the suggestions of the external developers.
4. External developers tend to determine the context for teaching curriculum units in a specified time sequence and in relation to other topics.	Teachers as user-developers may tend to accept the contextual decisions of external developers. Expert teachers with rich experience in teaching the specific topics and in-depth pedagogical content knowledge may be inclined to change the sequence and content linkages of curriculum units.

The main thrust of the second level of interpretation is the transformation of curriculum materials, which generally present content knowledge, into "forms that are pedagogically powerful and yet adaptive to the variations in ability and background presented by the students" (Shulman 1987, p. 15). This transformation is based on teachers' interpretation of materials, their ability to discern their potential, and their perception of reality. Reality, in this sense, encompasses the specific characteristics of a classroom, the students, their backgrounds, interests, prior knowledge, and conceptions and misconceptions, as well as the size of the class and its disposition for learning. Reality means the societal context in which learning takes place, the aims and concerns of parents and community, as well as the general ideological and economic framework. The teacher mentioned above, who was almost painfully aware of the sexist tone of the role card designations in the curriculum materials, acted on her perception of social reality. Her decision not to pay attention to the assignment of roles in the materials and to let the students make modifications in their role cards is an example of the impact of the perception of reality on teachers' curricular decisions.

Another component of reality concerns the constraints and limitations of resources which are available to teachers. A powerful example of resources is time. The lack of time is often perceived by teachers as *the* limiting factor in their ability to use the potential of curriculum materials. Fullan, in his book, *The Meaning of Educational Change* (1982), states the following: "Time is ignored because it is a problem that cannot be solved. There will never be enough of it" (p. 69). He draws our attention to the necessity of considering time seriously in all attempts to facilitate the teacher-curriculum encounter. The pressure of time is connected to teachers' concerns about curriculum coverage and to their ambivalent attitudes toward their role as curriculum creators.

CONCLUDING COMMENTS

It is argued that two processes of interpretation are involved in the transformation of content knowledge and ideas into learning settings. The preparation of curriculum materials based on scholarly knowledge is the first step in the long road to transforming knowledge into teachable and learnable forms. In this process the developers consider the educational potential which is implicit in the chosen content area. This potential may express itself in the information conveyed by the specific content. Important aspects of the educational potential of scholarly materials may also concern insights into the methods of inquiry leading to the acquisition of knowledge. Possible personal and societal meanings of knowledge are additional sources of educational potential considered by curriculum developers. As teachers plan their lessons, they engage in second-level interpretations and consider the variety of potential uses of the curriculum materials available to them. In this process teachers may "go back," so to speak, to the original questions asked by the developers, and decide to use the chosen components of subject matter in ways that were unintended by the originators of the curriculum materials. This examination of materials is critical for its adaptation to the reality of the educational situation. Two important matters need clarification.

1. How complex and rich in curriculum potential are the curriculum materials that teachers regularly use?
2. How can teachers' competence in interpreting the materials and in revealing a large variety of their potential uses be developed?

These matters will be dealt with in the next chapters in the context of a framework for enhancing teachers' expertise in curriculum interpretation and in uncovering curriculum potential by taking their own concerns into account.

RECOMMENDED ADDITIONAL READINGS

A paper which is enlightening from the point of view of curriculum potential is Reynolds et al. (1988): "Teachers and curriculum materials: Who is driving whom?" *Curriculum Perspectives* 8, 1:22–29.

Interesting insights into the intricacies of teacher planning and the need to adapt and supplement existing curriculum materials are provided by Gail McCutcheon's paper (1980): "How do elementary school teachers plan? The nature of planning and influences on it," *The Elementary School Journal* 81, 1:4–23.

There are several seminal writings regarding the notion of the hidden curriculum. The first is P. W. Jackson (1968): *Life in Classrooms*, New York, Holt, Rinehart and Winston. In her paper, "What should we do with a hidden curriculum when we find one?" (1976): *Curriculum Inquiry* 6, 2:135–151, Jane Martin analyzes the concept and its educational implications. David Gordon wrote a series of important articles on the topic of the hidden curriculum:

"The concept of the hidden curriculum" (1982): *Journal of Philosophy of Education* 16, 2:187–198; "The image of science, technological consciousness, and hidden curriculum" (1984): *Curriculum Inquiry* 14, 4:367–400; and "Education as text: The varieties of educational hiddenness" (1988): *Curriculum Inquiry* 18, 4:425–449.

The null curriculum is discussed in a paper by Flinders et al. (1986): "The null curriculum: Its theoretical basis and practical implications," *Curriculum Inquiry* 16, 1:33–42.

5

The Process
of Curriculum Interpretation

"You can't guard against the arbitrary"
Borkowski's law, in Paul Dickson,
The Official Rules, *1978, p. 17*

Chapter 4 discussed the concept of curriculum potential and its meaning for curriculum use by teachers. Curriculum interpretation was suggested as a way of revealing the potential of curriculum materials. This chapter provides some frameworks for interpretation and some concrete examples of products of interpretation efforts. We shall start with some distinctions regarding curriculum interpretation.

SUBJECTIVE AND OBJECTIVE MODES OF CURRICULUM INTERPRETATION

A useful distinction in the realm of curriculum interpretation is the distinction between *subjective* and *objective* modes of interpretation. The distinction between subjective and objective modes of inquiry has a long-standing philosophical tradition. Empirical-analytic sciences may be conceived as representing the objective inquiry mode. Popkewitz (1984) discusses the following characteristics of the empirical-analytic paradigm:

• Theory is to be universal and not bound to specific context.
• The empirical-analytic approach to inquiry is based on a commitment to distinterested science, independent of the goals and values of the people involved.
• The physical, biological, and social worlds are conceived as systems of variables which may be studied separately.
• There is a belief in formalized knowledge and operationalized concepts.

• Empirical-analytic research tends to rely on mathematics and quantification as a tool for theorizing.

Connelly and Clandinin (1988) argue that "traditionally we are taught to think of researchers and what they claim to know from their studies as being 'objective' " (p. 21). They go on to distinguish between this approach to knowledge and a "subjective" view, which is represented by narrative personal studies that focus on the past, present, and future of participating individuals. Such a notion of knowledge is concerned with its moral, emotional, and aesthetic dimensions.

From the point of view of the interpretation of the curricular text, Ricoeur's differentiation between "reading" and "philosophical interpretation" is considered important. "Reading" means the attempt to understand what is *in* the text, without imposing on it one's own convictions. "Philosophical interpretation," on the other hand, "goes on to take a position toward the work" (Ricoeur 1974, p. 160).

Gordon (1988), following Ricoeur, proposes the following distinction: "The orthodox view of the European school of hermeneutics has contrasted explanation and interpretation. Explanation is a notion borrowed from the natural sciences; interpretation is a form of 'verstehen'. Thus, in Ricoeur's view, explaining and interpreting a text are usually seen as the *objective* and *subjective* stances one can adopt toward the text" (p. 429).[10] (emphasis added)

This discussion brings us to the notion of 'maps' (Schumacher 1978). Schumacher talks about "maps of knowledge" which show the main ideas, pieces of information, and concepts we deem essential for our understanding of the world. Schumacher states that

> one way of looking at the world as a whole is by means of a map, that is to say, some sort of a plan or outline that shows where the various things are to be found—not all things, of course, for that would make the map as big as the world, but the things that are most prominent, most important for orientation: outstanding landmarks, as it were, which you cannot miss or which, if you do miss them, leave you in total perplexity. The most important part of any inquiry or exploration is its beginning. (Schumacher 1978, p. 15)

The beginning of "making a map" of a curricular text may be in the subjective or the objective mode. In the subjective mode personal knowledge and experiences serve as determinants of deciding what to look for and what to note as "landmarks" for our interpretation. In the objective mode we turn to categories, which stem from sources outside ourselves and which determine what to look for in the text. These objective maps may provide categories, or variables, for quantification, and may be independent of the special educational context of particular teachers.

Subjective interpretations, which are based on personal knowledge and experiences, may be impressionistic and intuitive, guided by implicit criteria and by stated or unstated assumptions. Interpretors may base their interpretations on analogies to previous experiences. Thus, a teacher may read a textbook passage dealing with stereotyping and view it as a powerful introduction to the social issues of minority groups. This interpretation may be traced back to a classroom discussion which was once generated by a text about discrimination. Another teacher may interpret the same passage as a possible starting point for dealing with sexist discrimination, basing this interpretation on her own personal experiences as a feminist.

Subjective and intuitive interpretations of curriculum materials are performed daily by teachers, who base their classroom activities on these interpretations. The math teachers mentioned in the previous chapter, who used nonverbal materials in geometry in order to generate storytelling, were probably moved to do so by their intuitive interpretation of these materials as providing stimuli for artistic activities. Because of their intuitive nature and their limitation to one's own personal experiences, subjective interpretations may not yield the whole richness of possible uses of any given set of curriculum materials. Objective interpretations, which are deliberately structured to reveal manifold aspects of curriculum materials, are therefore important in complementing the subjective mode of curriculum interpretation.

Objective interpretations are guided by predetermined categories of analysis which stem from sources other than the personal knowledge and experience of the interpretor. The use of structured schemes of curriculum analysis is a prerequisite for objective interpretation. Different persons using the same structured frames of analysis may arrive at similar characterizations of curriculum materials. Still, even these similar "curriculum profiles" may yield different modes of classroom use, according to the specific priorities and needs of the interpretors. Let us assume the following situation. A scheme of curriculum analysis which focuses on the linguistic complexity of texts reveals that a textbook in history is written in a highly complex language. Different teachers who become aware of this aspect of the curriculum materials may arrive at different conclusions. One, who believes that the students would benefit from learning about specific uses of language, might decide to spend time in history lessons on this issue. Another teacher, who believes that her students lack motivation to study history, might decide to devote her own time to writing historical tales which, though based on the textbook, present historical knowledge in a less complex language. Introducing objective modes of curriculum analysis does not mean that teaching will become uniform and will be carried out without attending to specific classroom situations and contexts. Rather, objective curriculum interpretation may provide teachers with frameworks for extending the use of existing curriculum materials in a more flexible manner. Through such interpretations teachers may reveal the educational potential of materials so that these may lend themselves to imaginative new uses.

FRAMES OF ANALYSIS

In order to carry out the objective interpretation of curriculum materials, frames of references are needed which may serve as sources for categories of analysis. For instance, one may decide to examine curriculum materials from the point of view of their implications for communication in the classroom. Such a theoretical frame has to be elaborated, and explicit categories for curriculum analysis have to be formulated. In the case of the communication framework, such categories may be "reading ease" and the "human interest" of the text (Flesh 1951). Another framework could be language seen as a vehicle for "transmission" versus language used mainly for "interpretation" (Barnes 1976). The "transmission" approach views language mainly as a medium for communicating ideas from teacher to pupil. The "interpretation" approach suggests that one has to reinterpret knowledge in order to possess it by trying to express it in one's own way. Such categories have to be further elaborated into a structured analytic system. For instance, Flesh (1951) has developed a system to arrive at a "complexity" score and a "human interest" score.

Curriculum interpretors who apply this system may become aware of inherent possibilities in curriculum materials which were not stated by their developers. For example, materials which are rated to have a high "human interest" score may be used to foster empathy in students. On the other hand, if teachers find that the curriculum text is lacking in this respect, they may overcome these curricular limitations by introducing additional materials into their teaching. This is another example of a null curriculum discussed in Chapter 4 and of its role in education.

INTERNAL AND EXTERNAL FRAMES OF REFERENCE

In the domain of objective interpretation, a further distinction can be made between internal and external frames of reference (Ben-Peretz 1981). *Internal frames of reference* originate in the rationale of curriculum developers. This rationale may state the intentions and objectives of the developers. An example of an objective of a curriculum unit in history may be that students will understand the function of historical sources and documents which serve as evidence and which are interpreted by historians in order to gain insights into past events (Adar and Fox 1978, p. 29). "Presentation of historical sources" may become a category for curriculum analysis. Several questions may stem from this category, for instance:

- How frequent is the use of historical sources in curriculum materials?
- What kind of historical sources are these?
- Does the text relate to the issue of the validity of historical sources?

We shall return later to some specific illustrations of the use of internal frames of reference for curriculum interpretations.

Let us turn now to *external frames of reference*, which are based on theoretical perspectives that are not part of the rationale of a curriculum unit. For instance, Kilbourn (1974) based his analysis of biology textbooks on the notion of scientific worldviews advanced by Pepper (1942). Pepper suggests that different views may serve "to make sense of the world." Among the worldviews that Pepper discusses are "mechanism" and "mysticism." Kilbourn used Pepper's theoretical perspective to reveal messages about "worldviews" which are projected by curriculum materials in biology. Such an aspect of curriculum materials is usually part of the hidden curriculum. Teachers and students may not be aware of the implied messages of the materials. The uncovering of these messages may have important implications for teaching. For instance, disclosing a "mechanistic" worldview in curricular materials may lead teachers to initiate classroom discussions about the nature of different worldviews and their impact on the development of science. This is an example of how the hidden curriculum, once disclosed, may be transformed deliberately into curriculum potential.

Analytic schemes based on specific theoretical frameworks have the power to illuminate diverse aspects of the analyzed materials and to provide important insights into their nature, yet the overall picture is necessarily incomplete. Different frames of reference leading to a variety of analytical schemes are bound to yield diverse and partial aspects of the complexity and richness of any set of curriculum materials. The interpretors who use these analytical schemes must be aware of the frames of reference guiding the collection and interpretation of data. Being conscious of these frameworks allows teachers to recognize, on the one hand, the special insights which they provide, and, on the other hand, to become sensitive to their limitations and possible shortcomings. For instance, Kilbourn's analytic scheme may be particularly helpful for teachers who think that it is important to acquaint their students with multiple worldviews which may be reflected in science curriculum materials. Some may believe that pointing explicitly to mysticism as a valid and defensible worldview may be meaningful in certain circumstances. Being aware of the conceptual basis of this analysis may also lead teachers to reject its usefulness as a guide for planning their lessons. They may conclude that this analytic scheme, although dealing with certain philosophical issues, does not relate to many other important aspects of the curriculum, such as the perception of learners implicit in the materials. What is needed, therefore, are diverse schemes of analysis which yield manifold insights into materials and extend teachers' grasp of their possible meanings and classroom uses.

How can teachers employ curriculum analysis and interpretation in their daily work? The following are some examples of subjective and objective modes of interpretation. We start with the presentation of two conceptual frameworks which may be useful for understanding teachers' subjective curriculum interpretation.

THE SUBJECTIVE MODE OF CURRICULUM INTERPRETATIONS

Subjective curriculum interpretation was defined as based on the personal knowledge and experiences of interpretors. Teachers assign meaning to the curriculum materials they use daily in their classrooms, and they try to comprehend and make sense of the innovative materials which they encounter in their teaching. Much of this sense making is subjective, guided by personal, idiosyncratic frames of reference. One way of viewing teachers' personal, idiosyncratic frames of reference is through the lenses of Kelly's personal construct theory (Ben-Peretz 1984).[11] Kelly's theory of personal constructs (Kelly 1955) may provide the conceptual framework for exploring teachers' own criteria for interpreting curriculum materials. According to Kelly's theory, human beings grasp their environment through the use of systems of personal constructs. At the root of this theory is the assumption that people strive to make sense of experience by construing and interpreting it in terms derived from individual past histories. A construct is essentially the particular basis for considering the way in which some things are seen as being alike and as different from others. Kelly likened constructs to sets of goggles through which persons view sections of the world, ordering them on the basis of personally meaningful characteristics. A construct is unlike a logical concept in that its boundaries are personally defined on the basis of individual and personal experience. Thus the construct "good" and its opposite pole, "not good," bear personal meaning for an individual beyond its logically defined sense. Fundamentally, Kelly's theory is a theory of human action, of an experiential cycle in which people develop their personal construct systems in interaction with their environment. Constructs may be considered forerunners of action. In the educational context, for instance, "the teacher who construes block building as an exercise for large muscle development will make different predictions about this activity, and undoubtedly act in different ways, from those who construe it as 'play,' or from another who construes it as the child's concrete representation of his thoughts" (Bussis et al. 1976, p. 17). Curriculum materials are part of the professional environment of teachers. From the point of view of Kelly's conceptual framework, teachers may be conceived as using personal constructs for examining, interpreting, and using available curriculum materials. These personal interpretations may then form the basis of teachers' lesson planning.

The following is an example of personal constructs which were generated by science teachers in their interpretation of the illustrations included in a biology textbook. These science teachers suggested a variety of constructs related to the illustrations, such as "motivating," "alienating," "cold," "attractive," and so forth. In the discussion which followed the generation of constructs, teachers elaborated the pedagogical implications of these constructs. Some teachers claimed that abstract figures provide opportunities for the conceptualization of biological phenomena. Others, who construed such illustrations as "cold," suggested that they might "turn students off." Teachers who had not conceived of illustrations in terms of "coldness" versus "warmth" were offered an opportunity to enrich their interpretations and to extend their perception of curriculum potential. This is but one example of subjective curriculum interpretation from the viewpoint of Personal Construct Theory. In Chapter 6 an instrument will be presented which may be used by teachers who are interested in uncovering their own personal constructs in relation to specific sets of curriculum materials.

A different view of teachers' personal frames of reference, which may help us understand subjective interpretations of curriculum materials, has been developed by Connelly and Clandinin (1985). They suggest that "the modes of knowing called forth by practitioners in teaching and learning situations are more properly understood, characterized and named in terms of narrative" (p. 183). For Connelly and Clandinin, "knowing is an experience." Action and knowledge are united in the actor, and our account of knowing is therefore of actors with their personal narratives and intentions. Connelly and Clandinin use the term *personal practical knowledge*, knowledge which is reconstructed out of the narratives of a person's life experiences. They present a narrative fragment, the "gingerbread boys episode," which exemplifies the experiential nature of a teacher's personal practical knowledge. This teacher made gingerbread boys with her class as a preparation for Christmas, arranging a display of cookies on a red velvet table cover. She insisted that the children be "good" and not eat the cookies until they had been hung on the Christmas tree. The authors state that "the knowing expressed in the gingerbread boys episode is an expression of Stephanie's personal practical knowledge of classrooms, in particular of her image of 'the classroom as home' and of her rhythm of teaching. The aesthetic and moral dimensions of the episode are rooted in these narratively grounded ways by which Stephanie knows her classroom" (Connelly and Clandinin 1985, pp. 187–188). In the case of this teacher, her image of the classroom determined the ways in which she planned for, and taught, in her classroom. The notion of narrative and the framework of the personal practical knowledge of teachers provide us with a view of teachers thinking about their curricula. Teachers' personal practical knowledge may account for their interpretations and uses of curriculum materials.[12]

THE OBJECTIVE MODE OF CURRICULUM INTERPRETATION

We turn now to two examples of objective modes of interpretation of curriculum materials, guided by predetermined categories of analysis.

First we'll amplify and illustrate the use of an *internal* analytic scheme, stemming from the rationale of the developers. For an example of the use of such an internal analytic scheme, we return to the work of Adar and Fox (1978) mentioned above. Adar and Fox analyzed the textbook and teachers' guide of a history curriculum, CM—*Lessons in History* (1974). Their categories for analysis were as follows:

- Use of historical sources as evidence for historical conclusions
- Actualization of historical events, namely, providing analogies between past events and present-day phenomena
- The moral aspects of historical episodes

The analysis by Adar and Fox serves to highlight congruencies and discrepancies between the rationale of the developers and the nature of the curriculum materials which are presented to teachers. More important, such an analysis may provide teachers with insights into the potential uses of the curriculum materials. A brief elaboration of the analysis, using one category only, is presented herewith.

Adar and Fox viewed the "use of historical sources" as reflecting the inquiry-oriented approach of the developers. This approach was expressed by the developers of the history unit (CM— Schavit et al 1974) as follows: "The teaching of history should impartknowledge about past events and develop insights into researchmodes which characterize history as a discipline" p. 196). The analytic scheme elaborated by Adar and Fox for the category of "use of historical sources" dealt with the following topics:

• Type of source: e.g., documents or illustrations of archeological findings
• Mode of presentation of source: e.g., with or without a
specific explanatory introduction
• Assigned function of the source in the textbook: e.g., as
part of the text or as evidence for statements in the text
• Extent of treating issues of source validity: e.g., not at
all, somewhat
• Extent of dealing with the nature of sources in the teachers' handbook

In their analysis Adar and Fox found that the textbook included
266 sources, most of which were illustrations of historical artifacts
and sections of documents. In 75 percent of all cases of presenting
historical sources, the developers wrote a brief introduction to the
source mentioning its background. Students were told, for instance, that knowledge about life in ancient Greece may be found
in the writings of Greek authors of that time, or that certain tools
were found on archeological sites.

As to the functions served by the sources, it was found that in
most cases the source was presented as a continuation or elaboration of the text. In very few cases sources were presented as evidence for some statements made by the text writers. Whenever the
function of sources as evidence is not clarified explicitly, students
and teachers may treat the source as part of the historical tale
which is told by the text. Thus the meaning of sources is distorted,
and their educational potential is not realized. Adar and Fox found
that the issue of source validity is only seldom treated in the student textbook and the teacher's handbook. The teacher's handbook treats the issue of source validity, in relation to only 6 percent
of all sources mentioned, in the context of guiding teachers in how
to deal with this issue in their lessons. In the summary the analysts state that they found the unit to be rich in historical sources.
In most cases the introduction to the source included some information regarding its time and origin, thus creating awareness of
the nature of historical sources. However, the function of sources
as evidence was hardly realized in the materials. Because of the
presentation of sources as a continuation or elaboration of the text,
students may tend to perceive sources as information which is
equal to the information imparted by the text instead of viewing
sources as evidence for the historical assertions made by the writ-

ers. The curriculum materials scarcely concern themselves with source validity, thus diminishing opportunities for developing insights into modes of historical research.

This example of curriculum interpretation based upon an *internal scheme of analysis* illustrates the use of curriculum interpretation to uncover curriculum potential. Teachers who become aware of this interpretation gain insights into the following features of this curriculum unit in history:

- The richness of the sources it contains
- The nature of these sources
- Weaknesses in the presentation of sources

The disclosed curriculum potential may serve teachers' lesson planning. Teachers may decide to devote part of their teaching time to the theme of "historical sources." They may plan to collect all sources which are presented in the students' textbook, to categorize them, and to discuss their validity and their role in historical research. Such learning experiences, which go beyond the suggestions made by the developers of this curriculum unit, may compensate for some of its weaknesses, enhancing the potential use of the materials. It is interesting to note that Adar and Fox (1978) found that only thirteen teachers out of the sixty-eight who taught the unit discussed the nature of the presented sources in their classrooms. It may well be that deliberate efforts of curriculum interpretation based on the kind of internal analysis applied by Adar and Fox would have resulted in different learning activities and in a larger number of teachers using the educational potential embodied in the historical sources which were part of the textbook.

You may try to analyze the curriculum materials you use, basing your analysis on some "internal" categories, such as the stated objectives of the developers.

EXTERNAL SCHEMES OF CURRICULUM ANALYSIS

"Curriculum analysis is the systematic examination of curricula with respect to a set of concrete concerns. This set of concerns, or scheme, is a conceptual framework that guides the analysis" (Ariav 1989, p. 194). Schemes of analysis aim at revealing the nature of curriculum materials, regardless of observed efforts of their use.

This focus on inherent qualities may provide insights into possible uses in practice. Eraut et al. (1975) define curriculum analysis as a set of questions designed for general application to curriculum materials in order to reveal their characteristics. External schemes of curriculum analysis provide such sets of questions, which are grounded in a conceptual framework that guides the analysis. Many schemes have been developed as instruments for systematic and deliberate analysis.[13]

Curriculum interpretations based on external schemes of analysis may disclose curriculum potential which was not anticipated by the developers. We shall start with the presentation of an external analysis scheme (Ben-Peretz 1977) which was based on Schwab's notion of curricular "commonplaces" (Schwab 1964). By "commonplaces" Schwab refers to the four main issues treated by curriculum developers in their development efforts, namely, subject matter, learner, milieu, and teacher. The rationale of this analytical scheme is based on the following assumptions about curriculum:

- Curriculum is an embodiment of developers' treatment of four factors: subject matter, learner, milieu, and teacher. Consideration of these four "commonplaces" in the process of curriculum development is assumed to be vital for defensible curricular deliberation and choice (Schwab 1973). Identification of the way these commonplaces are treated in curriculum materials is therefore considered to be a major task of curriculum analysis. If curriculum analysis reveals a pronounced lack of consideration of one of those factors—for instance, the special needs of anticipated students—teachers who use the materials may attempt to compensate for this deficiency in their own planning.
- Curriculum is viewed as the embodiment of educational potential. The potential of any given curriculum encompasses developers' intentions and suggested uses of the materials, as well as additional educational opportunities offered by the specific themes and topics treated in the materials.

The following is a brief description of the analytic scheme and its use in curriculum interpretation.

Subject matter, learner, milieu, and *teacher* constitute major dimensions for analysis. Each dimension is divided into a series of categories representing specific questions that may be asked about curriculum materials. The following are some examples of such categories. (A fuller description of this analytic scheme will be presented in Chapter 6: "Instruments and Procedures of Curriculum Interpretation.") In the *subject matter* dimension one of the categories of questions concerns approaches to scientific inquiry which are included in the materials. Schwab (1966) claims that honest statements of ignorance, uncertainty, and dubiety are conditions of human knowledge and should be included in curriculum materials in science. According to Schwab, the unique features of scientific research efforts have to be presented to students. In the *learner* dimension one category of questions relates to the anticipated learning styles of the students. This category is based on Hunt's (1974) notion of instruction and individual learning styles. Students are viewed as requiring different levels of structure in the learning environment. Since the nature of curriculum materials may determine the degree of structure experienced by students, a question about structure was included in the scheme. In the *milieu* dimension the analysis focuses on categories of possible interactions between society and the discipline being taught. Categories in the *teacher dimension* relate to the role expectation for teachers who may use the materials and to the consideration of teachers' needs. The last category is deemed important because considerations of teachers' needs may be ignored by curriculum developers, causing great difficulties in curriculum implementation (Leithwood 1976).

The emerging model of analysis is a matrix of four main dimensions that are conceived as being in a state of dynamic interaction; change in one could influence the others. For instance, a deliberate change in the treatment of subject matter could lead to new roles for teachers.

The scheme aims at revealing the complexity of curricular considerations and the richness of possible combinations. The scheme is descriptive and analytic, and is not to be considered a closed and prescriptive system of categories. Analysts using the scheme may adapt the use of categories to their specific needs, thus enriching the process of analysis and making it more flexible. Teachers may, for instance, decide to expand the milieu dimension because they consider this dimension to be crucial for their interpretation of curriculum materials. The results of the analysis have to be interpreted by teachers in the special context of their classroom situation.

We turn to an example of this scheme's application to two parallel chapters on respiration in two sets of curriculum materials in biology: "Respiration in Water" in *The Animal and Its Environment* (CM—1969) and "Respiration in Multicellular Organisms" in *Biological Science: An Inquiry into Life* (CM—1971). The main findings of the analysis (Ben-Peretz 1977) are presented herewith, accompanied with some interpretative comments.

The same biological principles are treated in both chapters, but with different emphases. In "Respiration in Multicellular Organisms" one finds some treatment of the unique nature of every scientific inquiry. This chapter draws attention to the place of scientists in scientific progress. Teachers may interpret the personal histories of the scientists included in the chapter as opportunities for dealing with the ability to overcome hardships and disappointments. Such an interpretation may fit their perception of student needs. In "Respiration in Water" there is no reference to the way scientific data are sought and interpreted. Scientists remain anonymous, and their background and methods of communication are not mentioned. On the other hand, this chapter deals with the interaction of science and the practical affairs of everyday life, an aspect that is absent in "Respiration in Multicellular Organisms." The two chapters differ in their treatment of the relationship between biology and other disciplines, such as chemistry or physics. This relationship is stressed in "Respiration in Multicellular Organisms" and is mentioned only seldom in "Respiration in Water."

Both chapters reflect to some extent an image of the learner as an "active inquirer" involved in guided discovery of biological principles, although both texts also transmit a large amount of information. The opportunities of learner development offered by both chapters are similar, "Respiration in Water" being richer in the variety of learning possibilities included. The two chapters are not intended for individualized instruction and are highly structured. The expression of the milieu dimension is not very pronounced. Of the variety of possible alternatives for treating the relationship between biology and society, one finds in "Respiration in Water" only some expression of the impact of society on the selection of scientific problems. "Respiration in Multicellular

Organisms" includes references to the historical background of research into respiration, thus offering teachers a possible starting point for discussing the interaction between society and biology.

There is a noticeable difference between the chapters regarding the teacher dimension. The teacher's guide accompanying "Respiration in Water" is rich in detailed instructions concerning instructional strategies, possibly restricting teachers' sense of autonomy in implementing the materials. The teacher's guide of "Respiration in Multicellular Organisms," on the other hand, leaves teachers a large degree of freedom in the selection of teaching strategies. In the context of these two chapters, teachers are offered only limited information about the deliberations of the developers which led to the construction of the materials. Lack of this information may limit the feasibility of defensible implementation. Teachers who are not aware of the underlying reason for decisions made by curriculum developers may find it difficult to reach valid decisions of their own about the materials. For instance, the developers may have decided to include certain items because they considered these to be interesting to students, thus enhancing their motivation to learn some specific topics. Teachers who are not informed about these considerations may tend to view the "motivating" items as components of knowledge which have to be transmitted to learners because of their cardinal importance as part of the subject matter structure. Neither chapter reflects consideration of teachers' needs, such as necessary knowledge of subject matter or time needed for preparation, even though these may be vital to the successful use of the materials.

The use of this scheme of analysis provides some examples of curriculum interpretation guided by a predetermined set of categories for analysis. The interpretation yields certain insights into the educational potential of the materials. For instance, teachers may decide to emphasize a certain unit in biology materials because it includes references to the historical background of the discipline, thus providing opportunities for relating to the interaction between society and the growth of science. The analysis of the two units on respiration revealed that both units are tightly structured and are not intended for individualized instruction. Teachers who interpret this structure to be unsatisfatory and who sense that their students would benefit from a more flexible and individualized instructional mode may have to change and modify the existing format of the materials. They may utilize potential starting points offered by the materials for transforming their classroom use.

In the use of this external analytic scheme we may distinguish between its possible functions in research and in educational practice. In research the scheme may be used to compare and review curriculum materials. Beyond that, the scheme may be used to provide data for gaining insights into curriculum trends in various subject matter areas across school systems and cultures. The organization of criteria in a structured system of categories allows the comparison of curricula and the determination of similarities and differences. In educational practice the scheme could fulfill a variety of functions. One of these functions is the selection, adoption, and adaptation of curriculum materials. Awareness of the characteristics of curriculum materials, as expressed in the curriculum profile constructed through using the analytic scheme, may serve the decision-making process of teachers. An enhanced understanding of the nature of curriculum materials provides teachers with the basis for defensible choices and adaptations. The analytic instrument may serve the process of curriculum implementation by creating awareness of the compatibility or incompatibility between basic characteristics of curriculum materials and specific educational situations. Thus, the profile of materials may be compared with teachers' perception and insights into the realities of their own classes. Appropriate changes in the curricular materials, using their educational potential, may be introduced on the basis of these comparisons.

You may wish to try and use this scheme to analyze a set of curriculum materials. If so, turn to the appendix, which presents the full instrument.

We have discussed two examples of objective interpretations, one based on an internal and one based on an external analytic scheme. We conclude this chapter with a brief account of one teacher's disclosure of the curriculum potential of a specific curriculum unit, based on the *unstructured "reading"* of the unit.

TEACHERS' READING OF CURRICULUM POTENTIAL

It has been argued so far that teachers would benefit from expertise in generating curriculum potential and for suggesting divergent ways for using curricular items. Teachers must be able to link these suggestions to anticipated possible outcomes and to specific learner populations and individual learners. The richness of perceived curriculum potential will be determined by teachers' expertise in the subject matter area, their past teaching experiences, their feeling for classroom reality, and, last but not least, their interpretative abilities.

The following is an example of teachers' reading of curriculum potential without a framework of predetermined categories. This example is based on the responses of experienced teachers who were asked to suggest divergent possible uses of one particular curriculum item (Ben-Peretz et al. 1977). The item relating to a learning activity was taken from a textbook on environmental studies for junior high school: "List as many detergents for cleaning and washing as you can. You may find different varieties in a supermarket. In your list note the name of the product, its composition and its uses" (Ben-Peretz et al. 1977, p. 34). After concluding their lesson planning based on this curricular item, the participating teachers were interviewed about the process of generating ideas for multiple uses of curriculum items. They were asked about possible sources for their ideas, their past experiences with similar learning activities, and their reasons for making their suggestions. Figure 2 is a graphic representation of the responses of one experienced teacher.

The overall goal for slow learners, as defined by this teacher, was to raise their awareness of the complexity of environmental phenomena "so that they won't accept their environment as 'given', without thinking about it." The overall goal for regular students was "to develop a critical stance toward industrial products," to raise awareness of students to the fact "that every good thing has its disadvantages." The teacher seems to be most sensitive to the perceived needs of the slow learners in her class. This sensitivity leads her to change the nature of the specified curricular task. Instead of involving the shelves of the supermarket, the task becomes home oriented, because the teacher thinks that the prescribed task is too difficult for certain students. A variety of follow-up tasks for slow learners are planned by the teacher, mostly in the practical context of uses of detergents (how effective they are, what damage they may cause, how much they cost). It is interesting to note that the topic is perceived by the teacher as a stimulus for experiments for *all* her students. The laboratory ap-

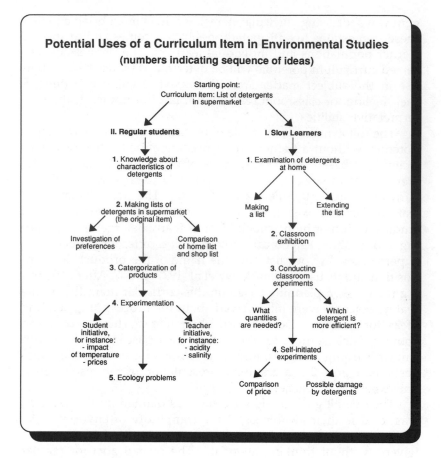

Potential Uses of a Curriculum Item in Environmental Studies
(numbers indicating sequence of ideas)

Starting point:
Curriculum item: List of detergents
in supermarket

II. Regular students

I. Slow Learners

1. Knowledge about
characteristics of
detergents

1. Examination of detergents
at home

Making
a list

Extending
the list

2. Making lists of
detergents in supermarket
(the original item)

2. Classroom
exhibition

Investigation of
preferences

Comparison
of home list
and shop list

3. Conducting
classroom
experiments

3. Catergorization of
products

What
quantities
are needed?

Which
detergent is
more efficient?

4. Experimentation

Student
initiative,
for instance:
- impact
of temperature
- prices

Teacher
initiative,
for instance:
- acidity
- salinity

4. Self-initiated
experiments

5. Ecology problems

Comparison
of price

Possible damage
by detergents

proach seems to be deeply ingrained in this science teacher. The teacher distinguishes between experiments planned by her ("I would sit down and plan experiments for each group of products") and experiments initiated by the students ("I would ask for, even demand, suggestions for experiments. Problems of the impact of heating the water for laundry, for instance, can be raised by all students"). The potential of this curricular unit was developed differentially for regular and for slow learners in the class, even though the unit itself does not call for such a differentiation. The teacher assumes that her "regular" students require some prerequisite knowledge about detergents before starting work on the unit. Extending the theoretical basis of chemical knowledge seems to her to be an appropriate elaboration of the curriculum potential embodied in the unit. Only the regular students are required to survey detergents in supermarkets, and only they are expected to dwell on the ecological issues raised by the widespread use of detergents. The teacher differentiates between students not only in the realm of assigned learning activities, but even in the realm of curricular "messages." Whereas the regular students are expected to acquire a "critical stance," slow learners are expected to "become more aware of the complexity of the world."

It is not our intention to evaluate this differentiation. The episode was elaborated to show how teachers do, in fact, derive educational possibilities from existing curricular units. This episode may be viewed as a case for further reflection by teachers on their own implicit assumptions in the process of developing the potential of curriculum units. Structured "external" schemes of analysis could be helpful in this respect. Further reflection could lead, conceivably, to changes in their plans for using the curriculum materials. Ben-Peretz et al. (1977) found that experienced teachers differ from student-teachers and novices in their approach to the process of generating curriculum potential. Experienced teachers start with general ideas and only then turn to elaboration and specification of classroom activities. Student-teachers and novices tend to start with highly specific ideas. This difference in procedures of generating curriculum potential may partly account for the greater productivity of experienced teachers which was revealed in this study.

You may try to compare the elicitation of curriculum potential of experienced and novice teachers. Group discussions of such efforts could serve to enhance the scope of identified uses of materials of both experienced and novice teachers.

CONCLUDING COMMENTS

Chapter 5 starts with some distinctions which are considered relevant for the process of curriculum interpretation. First, subjective and objective interpretations of materials are contrasted. Then the distinction between internal and external schemes of analysis are discussed. Several examples of these different approaches to curriculum interpretation are presented, and their use in revealing curriculum potential is elaborated. The chapter concludes with a consideration of expert teachers' elicitation of curriculum potential. The pedagogical reasoning model of Shulman assumes "that content knowledge is influential in realizing curriculum potential" (Gudmunsdottir and Shulman 1986, p. 443). It is suggested that a solid body of pedagogical content knowledge, of the kind necessary to reveal curriculum potential, distinguishes the experienced from the novice teacher. This body of pedagogical content knowledge allows teachers to interpret curriculum materials in order to generate their potential for classroom use. Pedagogical content knowledge, according to Shulman (1987), blends content and pedagogy into an understanding of how to organize particular topics and to present them for instruction in diverse teaching situations. It is our claim that the planned cultivation of curriculum interpretation abilities is extremely important for the generation of curriculum potential, and that development of these abilities may serve to extend the pedagogical content knowledge of teachers.

The next chapter will present, exemplify, and discuss specific instruments and procedures of curriculum interpretation that may be used by teachers in their attempts to disclose the educational potential of curriculum materials.

RECOMMENDED ADDITIONAL READINGS

David Gordon's article (1988): "Education as text: The varieties of educational hiddenness," *Curriculum Inquiry* 18, 4:425–449, develops the ideas of Ricoeur in his search for hidden meanings of text and presents Gordon's analysis of the hidden curriculum. This article also provides important insights into the philosophical distinction between objective and subjective stances that can be adopted toward texts.

Chapter 1 (pp. 9–23) of E. F. Schumacher's (1977) *A Guide for the Perplexed*, London, Cox and Wyman, deals with philosophical maps and with the question of truth, and could be of interest to a reader who wants to get a view of subjective or objective aspects of inquiry.

The book *Teachers as Curriculum Planners: Narratives of Experience* by F. M. Connelly and D. J. Clandinin (1988), New York, Teachers College Press, and Toronto, OISE Press, offers readers a view of curriculum within schools by seeking to understand teacher planning through the use of teachers' narratives.

Readers who are not familiar with Kelly's personal construct theory and its significance for education may find the book *Personal Construct Psychology and Education* by M. Pope and T. Keen (1981), London, Academic Press, very helpful.

A seminal work regarding curriculum analysis schemes is Eraut, M., Goad, L., and Smith, G. (1975): *The Analysis of Curriculum Materials*, Educational Area, Occasional Papers 2, Brighton, University of Sussex. Another source for reading about curriculum analysis schemes is the chapter by M. Ben-Peretz, "Curriculum analysis as a tool of evaluation" (1981), in A. Lewy and D. Nevo (eds.), *Evaluation Roles in Education*, London, Gordon and Breach.

6

Instruments and Procedures
of Curriculum Interpretation

"When we try to pick out anything by itself we find it
hitched to everything else in the universe"
Muir's Law

A. Block, Murphy's Law Book Two, *1985 p. 96*

The previous chapters provided the rationale and conceptual
framework for enhancing teachers' abilities in curriculum interpretation. This chapter presents several instruments and the accompanying procedures which were developed for this purpose.
These instruments and procedures exemplify some of the distinctions made in Chapter 5, namely, the distinction between subjective and objective interpretation, and the distinction between
external and internal frames of reference for analysis and interpretation.

The presentation of these instruments aims at providing teachers and anyone interested in curriculum materials with tools for curriculum inquiry. Curriculum inquiry means, in the context of this
book, the process of uncovering the meaning of curricular texts
used by teachers. These texts are mainly in the form of teacher
guidelines and handbooks, student textbooks, and supplementary
instructional materials. Curricular texts may be read on their own
terms in order to find out what intentions were built into the materials by their developers. This kind of reading may be supported
by the "internal" schemes of analysis which are exemplified in this
chapter. Another way of reading is based on the readers' terms,
using one's own frame of reference to uncover the personal meaning of the text. One of the instruments in this chapter provides the
reader with a tool for revealing the personal meanings of curricular
texts. The "external" scheme of analysis presented in this chapter
provides a way of recovering the meaning of a curricular text
through the lenses of deliberately chosen categories of analysis.

The reader may try to use the different instruments by asking himself or herself, what is the meaning of the curriculum materials from different points of view? Following this question it is important to ask oneself, considering my understanding of the materials, how can I use them in my own classroom?

Four instruments will be presented and discussed:

1. The Curriculum Item Repertory (CIR), which was developed by Ben-Peretz et al. (1982). This instrument serves to identify the personal constructs of teachers which they use for interpreting curriculum materials. As was argued above, "personal constructs" represent one possible conceptual framework of idiosyncratic, subjective frames of reference for making sense of one's environment, in this case of curriculum materials.

2. A scheme for syllabus analysis which was developed by Silberstein and Ben-Peretz (1983). This scheme is intended for the interpretation of curriculum outlines and guidelines for teachers. It is an example of the objective mode of curriculum interpretation based on an internal perspective.

3. A scheme for analysis of curriculum materials, that is, student textbooks and teacher handbooks, developed by Ben-Peretz (1977). This is another example of an objective scheme, reflecting an "external" perspective. The framework adopted for analysis is based on Schwab's (1964) notion of curricular "commonplaces," namely, subject matter, learner, milieu, and teacher.

4. The matching wheel, developed by Ben-Peretz and Lifmann (1978), an instrument which may serve curriculum interpretation in both the internal and external objective modes.

THE CURRICULUM ITEM REPERTORY (CIR)

This instrument is an extension of the Role Construct Repertory Test form and is based on the triadic sorting methodology for the individual elicitation of personal constructs. Respondents are asked to relate to a set of "elements" which serve as objects for construct elicitations. Examples of elements are the students in a teacher's classroom, types of educational innovations, television programs, or a list of books. Although Kelly (1955) developed his theory within the field of psychotherapy, it is applicable to many settings. People are conceived as construing the various aspects of reality. Their constructs are the result of the personal interpretation of their world. A construct is a way in which some elements are perceived as being alike and different from other elements. It is therefore essentially two-ended, involving a particular basis for considering likenesses and differences. In triadic sorting, respondents are asked to relate to triads of elements, deciding for each triad which two elements are alike and which one is different according to a criterion suggested by them. These differentiating criteria constitute their constructs for relating to these specific elements, which are part of their environment.

The CIR instrument consists of a set of twenty curriculum items selected from a set of curriculum materials. These items include passages from a student textbook, illustrations, and so forth. The items function as elements for eliciting constructs. Each curriculum item is glued to a card, and all cards are assigned a letter. Fifteen elements, in this case fifteen cards of curriculum items, are a suitable number of elements for construct elicitation purposes. Different triads of elements are formed and presented to teachers, for example, an illustration, a passage of text, and a learning activity. The elicitation of constructs by teachers starts with the sorting of these triads, deciding for each triad which two are similar and different from the third, according to a self-determined criterion. For example, one teacher may decide that the textbook passage and the learning activity are similar because both focus on certain intellectual skills, whereas the illustration is different, having mainly an emotional impact. The basis for similarity is called the "emerging pole" of the construct. The contrasting characteristic is called the "contrast pole" of the construct. The two poles of the construct, in this case, will be fostering intellectual skills/not fostering intellectual skills. Another teacher, sorting the same triad, may decide that the learning activity and the illustration are similar, both being potentially motivating for student learning, whereas the textbook passage is different, lacking the power to motivate. The two poles of the construct in this case will be motivating/not motivating.

Each criterion suggested by teachers is conceived as representing a personal construct which serves teachers in their interpretation of curriculum materials. Altogether fifteen different triads are to be sorted. All constructs are noted on a grid form. The grid form has the letters of elements written horizontally on top. At the left-hand side of the form are two columns, one for noting the composition of items composing each triad, and one for noting the emerging pole of the construct, the basis for similarity. In the column at the right-hand side, the contrast pole of the construct, one notes the characteristic which determines the dissimilarity.

After a construct for each triad is produced, all the elements on the grid are rated on a 5-point scale to reflect where each element lies between the two poles of the elicited construct. Each construct chosen by a teacher for sorting the elements of any triad is then used for classifying all other elements, all other curriculum items listed on the grid. For example, a teacher may use the two poles of a construct, motivating/not motivating, which were elicited by one triad, to classify all the cards of curriculum items. Items which are perceived by the teacher as highly motivating will be rated with a 5. Items which are perceived as nonmotivating, representing the contrast pole of the construct, will be rated a 1. Items which are in between, according to the teacher's judgments, will be rated 3.

Figure 3 is an example of a completed grid filled out by one respondent. Scanning the grid presented in Figure 3, one may see that different triads elicited different constructs. For instance, triad ABC elicited the construct motivating/not motivating. Elements A and B were rated 5, motivating. Element C was rated 1—not-motivating. The same construct was used by the respondent to rate elements D and E which were not part of the first triad. Each element is a curriculum item as specified in Figure 3. Element D was rated 4, a little less motivating than A or B. Element E was rated 2 not-motivating, but slightly less so than element C.

One should remember that the rate of 5 means closest to the positive pole, whereas the rate of 1 means closest to the contrast pole. The second triad, BCD, elicited the construct difficult/not difficult. All elements which are perceived as being difficult were rated 5, those which were perceived as being not difficult were rated 1. One can perceive the nature of any curriculum item as construed by the respondent who constructed this grid by scanning the grid vertically. For example, item E, the encyclopedic passage, was perceived by the respondent as being not motivating, difficult, not suitable for independent learning, allowing no expression of emotions, and having no potential for group activity. On the other hand, item D, a story about personal experiences,

Example of a Shortened Version of a Completed Curriculum Item Repertory (CIR) Grid

The following elements are curriculum items in biology relating to the hydrodynamic form

A. Two illustrations, one showing a rider on a horse and one a rider on a motorcycle

B. A short textbook paragraph on the hydrodynamic form in technology

C. A series of textbook questions related to the hydrodynamic form

D. A student activity requiring a story about personal experiences related to the hydrodynamic form

E. An encyclopedic item on the development of motor vehicles

Composition of triads	Elements	A	B	C	D	E	
	Construct (positive pole)						Construct (contrast pole)
ABC	Motivating	5	5	1	4	2	Not motivating
BCD	Difficult	1	5	5	1	5	Not difficult
CDE	Independent learning activity	3	3	5	1	5	No independent learning activity
ACE	Illustrations	5	1	1	1	5	No illustrations
ABD	Expression of emotions	5	1	1	5	1	No expression of emotions
BCE	Potential for group activity	1	5	5	5	1	No potential for group activity

was perceived as motivating, not difficult, allowing expression of emotions, and highly suitable for group activity but not for independent learning. One may also derive some relationships between constructs by scanning the grid horizontally. For instance, the constructs "motivating" and "expression of emotions" are perceived as closely linked. Any item considered motivating is considered in most cases to allow for the expression of emotions, in this case items A and D. Item B is an exception, it is considered to be motivating but not providing opportunities for the expression of emotions. Items C and E are perceived as being not-motivating and not providing opportunities for the expression of emotions. Such a scanning of grids may provide teachers with insights into their perception of curriculum materials. Comparing one's own constructs with the constructs of other teachers may extend one's own understanding of the educational potential of materials. The CIR instrument provides insights into some of the personal meanings assigned by teachers to curriculum materials. Discussing constructs with one's peers and colleagues is a possible strategy for enhancing and enriching the interpretative abilities of teachers.

One example of the possible educational implications of such a discussion, related to textbook illustrations, was presented in the previous chapter. Another example is taken from a triadic sorting experience of curriculum items in English. Some of the participants were experienced teachers, and some were novices. The constructs generated by experienced teachers tended to focus on methods of teaching, for example, "expository versus inquiry teaching," and on the required cognitive abilities, such as "comprehension versus rote learning." Constructs generated by novice teachers tended to be in the realm of language structure, for example, "prepositions," or students' tasks, such as "writing assignment versus oral work" (Ben-Peretz et al. 1982). Although no two personal construct systems are alike, similarities between groups of people may exist because people may inhabit similar external worlds (Bannister 1970). In the ensuing discussion teachers became aware of the possible extensions in their thinking about curriculum materials. Some of the pedagogical implications of the various ways of construing materials were considered.

The CIR instrument may be used individually or in groups by teachers who are interested in uncovering the underlying constructs which provide the basis for attaching meaning to the curriculum materials they use in their classroom.

Curriculum items which serve as elements for construct elicitations may be chosen at random from a set of curriculum materials. In that case the instrument reveals the personal constructs of teachers relating to diverse curriculum materials. Items may also be chosen deliberately to represent the possible characteristics of a set of materials. In that case the instrument reveals how teachers construe those specific characteristics, such as learning by discovery.

You may wish to make up your own grid by choosing elements of a set of curriculum materials you use. Reflect on your constructs and about what you can learn about your personal "reading" of curriculum materials. What are some of the educational implications of your interpretation based on your personal constructs? You may try to cooperate with your colleagues, each of you creating his or her own grid and then discussing your different "readings" of the curricular text.

A SCHEME FOR ANALYZING SYLLABI AND TEACHER GUIDELINES

This scheme is based on a curriculum perspective which views the construction of curriculum materials as being guided by the "platform" of its developers (Walker 1974). This platform constitutes a system of values, beliefs, and opinions about what is possible and desirable from an educational viewpoint. The platform may be reflected in the syllabi prepared by curriculum developers for teachers' use. As stated in Chapter 2, syllabi usually consist of an outline of a course of study specifying the themes or topics of a subject matter area. Sometimes the syllabus entails several distinguishable parts: a list of topics and themes, goals and objectives, suggestions for instructional strategies, and sometimes even the underlying rationale of the developers.

The question arises whether it is important to convince teachers that knowing and using the rationale formulated in the syllabus is really necessary. Is it not more important and valuable that teachers plan their lessons independently of admonitions of the syllabus, using their own knowledge of subject matter and classrooms as the basis of their teaching? Teacher autonomy is indeed deemed crucial for designing ways of teaching which will reach the mind and heart of every student, yet teachers do not practice in a vacuum; syllabi and teacher guides exist and are important resources to be used wisely and appropriately.

Our basic assumption is that the implementation process of curriculum by its very nature has to be an open, adaptive, ramifying process (Ben-Peretz 1975). This view is congruent with the "mutual adaptation" approach described by Fullan and Pomfret (1977). According to this approach, the process has to be adaptive to the diverse needs of the target population, to the diversity of teaching cirumstances, and to teachers' personal educational philosophy. Only teachers who are conscious of the conceptual framework of a particular curriculum are capable of seeing the boundaries of the "curriculum envelope" of this curriculum, mentioned in Chapter 2 (Bridgham 1971). Teachers who are able to read a syllabus critically are in a position to accept or to reject some, or even all, of the specific characteristics of the curriculum. Peters (1967) argues that "failure to grasp underlying principles leads to unintelligent rule of thumb application of rules and the inability to make exceptions on relevant grounds and to bewilderment in novel situations" (p. 6).

The following structured questions may assist teachers in their analysis of a syllabus or of teacher guidelines:

1. What are the major parts of the syllabus, such as the following?
   a. A list of topics or themes
   b. Recommended sequences and/or time specifications for teaching these topics or themes
   c. Recommended teaching strategies
2. What is the rationale of the curriculum, as stated by its developers? The rationale may include statements about the following:
   a. The nature of the subject matter
   b. How the subject matter is related to other disciplines
   c. The relation of the program to general or specific educational goals
   d. Suggested teaching strategies and their appropriateness for different student population
   e. The anticipated role of teachers using the materials

This first step in syllabus analysis reveals which issues were dealt with by the developers and which were left open. For instance, a syllabus may be highly specific regarding the topics to be covered by the teacher and students, yet may leave the sequencing and time allocations open for teachers' decisions. A set of teacher guidelines may include elaborate discussions about the nature of the subject matter and its connections to other disciplines but may be silent about the anticipated student population. Teachers who are aware of these specifications or omissions may be in a better position to plan their courses on the basis of the syllabus, for instance, through trying to match the specified content with a target audience.

It is considered important for teachers to be aware of the messages transmitted by curriculum developers, not necessarily in order to accept them, but in order to be able to consider carefully the possible uses of the curriculum in their classrooms.

In the second step in syllabus analysis teachers analyze specific statements in the rationale relating to the following questions:

1. What is the nature of the subject matter as conceived by the developers? Statements about the main features of the body of knowledge, its structure, and modes of inquiry may be found in a syllabus or in teachers' guidelines. For example:

   GEOGRAPHY
   Introduction
   This unit focuses on Geography, the study of the planet Earth and its peoples. Geography is divided into several disciplines: physical geography, cultural geography, economic geography, and strategic geography.

   Geographic concepts you will be teaching as part of this unit include:
   • Geography: its nature and scope
   • System and ecosystem; closed and open systems
   • The First World; The Second, Third, and Fourth Worlds
   • Interdependence
   • Map: scale, direction, legend; Globe
   • Physical, political geography
   • Gross National Product
   • Strategic resources
   • Global and national development
   • Time; Space

Geographic processes and skills you will be teaching as part of this unit include:
- Analyzing a system
- Making maps and interpreting existing maps
- Determining time zones
- Role-playing and simulation
- Abstracting and condensing information
- Getting information from graphs, tables and charts

This unit, as the others in the text, is constructed to maximize student development in learning basic processes and concepts in the social sciences and to facilitate a creative teacher-student working environment. (CM—Bonstingel 1985, p. 157)

2. How is the subject matter domain related to other disciplines? One may find, for instance, that the subject matter is considered a prerequisite for other areas of study, or that it is viewed as integrated with other domains. For example:

We do not see "People and Resources" as a school subject on its own. It is a collection of materials which can be used in a variety of contexts. For example, it can be used with topics already included in established school subjects such as biology, chemistry, physics, integrated science, social studies, geography, history, environmental studies, etc. (CM—"People and Resources," 1975, p. 8)

3. What is the expected relation of the curriculum to educational goals? Developers tend to determine the goals of their programs. For example:

To provide information and experience by which students would gain appreciation of some of the diverse ways in which people both affect and are affected by the use of natural resources. (CM—"People and Resources," 1975, p. 7)

4. What are the recommended modes of teaching and learning? Sometimes these are derived from the perceived nature of the discipline. For example:

The students should demonstrate an inquiry approach to biology and be able to design and carry out simple experiments with living organisms. (CM—"Man and Water," 1975, p. 2)

5. What is the anticipated role of teachers in the program? Syllabi and curriculum guidelines may be quite specific about these roles. For example, the role of the teacher is

that of an organizer and guide, ensuring the smooth running of the investigations, pointing to follow-up work and links with other subjects, acting as chairman for discussions, summarizing the results of a piece of work, sorting out the difficulties of individual students and so on. (CM—"People and Resources," 1975, p. 9)

The syllabus may be quite explicit regarding recommended sequences and time allocations. For example:

The books can be used in any order and there is something to be said for using them over several successive years, say one book for part of a year over a period of three years. . . . (CM—"People and Resources," 1975, p. 8)

Sometimes the syllabus may not be as clear in its statements, and teachers who search for answers to these questions may have to interpret implicit messages of the text. The syllabus may not be explicit regarding the structure of knowledge of the content domain. For instance, a teacher reading the following passage may find it difficult to translate it to classroom teaching.

The content of an Environmental Education curriculum will have much in common with thematic and subject-matter areas, particularly values, careers and consumer education as well as the subject areas of science, mathematics, social studies, language arts and the fine arts. What is attempted here is the drawing of a map of the domain of Environmental Education along with suggestions for methods to develop a comprehensive curriculum. (CM—Department of Education, Hawaii 1977, p. 7)

In this case teachers have to develop their own interpretations of the nature of a "map" of the domain of
environmental education.

Teachers who wish to be autonomous implementors of ready-
made curriculum guidelines may find an analysis guided by the
questions posed above useful in their daily work. Conducting the
analysis in groups, teachers may experience different ways of
identifying assumptions and considerations related to various aspects of the rationale. Teachers who are conscious of the conceptual framework of a particular curriculum may be able to decide
deliberately whether to remain within the boundaries of this curriculum. Relating the findings of the analysis to specific situations
constitutes an integral and important part of teachers' reflecting
about curriculum.

*You may wish to try to use the questions posed above in order to
reveal the inherent characteristics of your curriculum materials.*

A SCHEME FOR ANALYZING CURRICULUM MATERIALS (STUDENT TEXTBOOKS AND/OR TEACHERS' HANDBOOKS)

This scheme was described in Chapter 5, and its use in revealing
curriculum characteristics was demonstrated there. We turn now
to a fuller presentation of this analytic instrument. The Curriculum
Analysis Matrix (Ben-Peretz 1977) consists of four basic dimensions: subject matter, learner, milieu, and teacher. These dimensions are presented here with examples for each category in each
dimension. The worksheet format of this instrument is included in
the appendix. In the worksheets each statement of the instrument
can be rated as representing the curriculum materials in the following way:

1—not at all
2—somewhat
3—to a large extent

Thus "profiles" of curriculum materials can be drawn up. The
various statements in each category reflect possible curricular orientations in each dimension.

Dimension No. 1: Subject Matter

This dimension relates to the expression of different orientations, to "subject matter" that can be identified in curriculum materials. Five categories of analysis are proposed, as follows:

Category 1.10. Information, concepts, principles

> 1.11. The materials present specific information, e.g.: The largest of sequoia trees is called General Sherman.
> 1.12. The materials emphasize unifying concepts, e.g.: The leaves are covered by an epidermis.
> 1.13. The materials emphasize general principles, e.g.: Living organisms need oxygen.

Category 1.20. Approaches to the nature of scientific inquiry

> 1.21. The materials imply the existence of a general mode of inquiry, e.g.: Scientists use controls in their experimentation.
> 1.22. The materials present specific methodologies for different research problems, e.g.: Special methods of inquiry are needed to investigate animal coloring.

Category 1.30. Relationship to everyday life

> 1.31. The materials convey the meaning of subject matter knowledge for individuals, e.g.: You sit in your room at night, reading, and suddenly the light goes out. Which of your senses will help you to find your way?
> 1.32. The materials express the meaning of subject matter knowledge for society, e.g.: The potato blight catastrophe in Ireland may be used to explain the impact of plant diseases on human migration.

Category 1.40. Image of scientist

> 1.41. Scientists and scholars are mentioned anonymously, e.g.: Scientists discovered that fish are able to breathe if there are green plants in the water.
> 1.42. Scientists and scholars are mentioned by name, e.g.: Archimedes' Law is presented.
> 1.43. The personal background of scholars is described, e.g.: Spallazani was a jurist by education, a priest by vocation, and an ardent biologist by inclination.

Category 1.50. Integration with other disciplines

1.51. The materials present knowledge from various disciplines as a prerequisite for understanding, e.g.: You may remember that water molecules may be separated through electrolysis.

1.51. The materials present transfer of knowledge from one discipline to another, e.g.: Knowledge about the hydrodynamic forms serves engineering.

Dimension No. 2: Learner

This dimension relates to the expression of different orientations to the "learner" that can be identified in curriculum materials. Four categories of analysis are proposed, as follows:

Category 2.1. Image of learner

2.11. The learner is involved in active discovery learning, e.g.: Is rain water similar to tap water? Plan experiments to investigate this question.

2.12. The learner is expected to acquire knowledge that is presented in the textbook, e.g.: Note that many animals living in deep waters possess some light equipment for recognition of species members, as well as for the search for food.

Category 2.20. Opportunities for learner development

2.21. The materials offer opportunities for cognitive development, e.g.: Try to explain the relationship between the surface area of lungs and the intensity of breathing.

2.22. The materials offer opportunities for affective involvement, e.g.: Try to imagine the impact of hunger on the behavior of animals in captivity.

2.23. The materials offer opportunities for psychomotor development, e.g.: Use small pincers to transfer cuts of leaves to a Petri dish.

Category 2.30. Intended focus of instruction

2.31. The learner is perceived as an individual with particular needs and interests, e.g.: The materials suggest varied ways to study one specific topic.

2.32. The learner is perceived as a member of a group with shared interests and needs, e.g.: Common learning tasks are suggested for all students.

Category 2.40. Learning style

2.41. The learner is perceived as being able to function in a variety of learning environments, structured or unstructured, e.g.: Unstructured learning tasks, such as unguided observations of birds, are included in the text.

2.42. The learner is perceived as requiring a highly structured learning environment, e.g.: Step-by-step directions for carrying out an experiment are provided.

Dimension No. 3: Milieu

This dimension relates to the influences of society on the growth of the subject matter being taught, as well as to the impact this subject matter has on society. Another aspect of milieu relates to the impact of society on the way subject matter is treated in the curriculum.

Category 3.10. Interaction between society and the discipline

3.11. Influences of society on the development of the discipline are explicitly mentioned in the materials, e.g.: Stories about the impact of Marxist ideology on the development of genetics are included in the materials.

3.12. Influences of the development of the discipline on society are explicitly mentioned in the materials, e.g.: The growth of "marine farms" for future modes of agriculture is discussed.

Category 3.20. Interaction between society and the process of curriculum development

3.21. Curriculum materials reflect societal needs, e.g.: Curricula in environmental studies; black studies; women studies; Holocaust studies.

3.22. Curriculum materials reflect ideological concerns, e.g.: Inclusion of the story of creation alongside a text about evolution.

Dimension No. 4: Teacher

This dimension relates to the role expectations for teachers in the process of curriculum development, implementation, and evaluation. Four categories for analysis are proposed. The objects of analysis are teacher guides and manuals.

Category 4.10. Communication of developers' considerations to teachers

4.11. The teachers' guide relates developers' considerations regarding selection of subject matter, e.g.: The relationship between structure and function is emphasized in the materials because this concept is central for explaining many of life's phenomena.
4.12. The teachers' guide explains the rationale of the developers regarding students, e.g.: Explanations of the motivational meaning of various themes and learning activities are given.
4.13. The teachers' guide deals explicitly with developers' considerations regarding the milieu in which the curriculum is to be implemented, e.g.: Multicultural themes are included because of the ethnic composition of target populations.
4.14. The teachers' guide discusses anticipated roles for teachers implementing the materials, e.g.: Teachers are required to initiate group activities in teaching.

Category 4.20. Degree of teacher autonomy

4.21. Specific objectives are stated, e.g.: Students will be able to read and comprehend scientific texts in biology.
4.22. Teaching strategies are specified, e.g.: Students will work in homogeneous groups.
4.23. Background materials are included in the curriculum package, e.g.: Scientific articles about water pollution are part of the environmental education curriculum package.
4.24. Teachers are offered teaching alternatives, e.g.: Three different themes related to the human nervous system are included in the curriculum.
4.25. Teachers are advised to develop their own units, e.g.: certain topics are not included in the curriculum materials, and it is suggested that teachers develop their own units.

Category 4.30. Teachers' role in instruction

4.31. The materials suggest a central role for teachers as sources of subject matter knowledge, e.g.: Teachers are required to provide students with certain information.

4.32. The materials suggest a supportive role for teachers who guide their students in independent learning, e.g.: Teachers are required to insist on active cooperation of students in experimentation, discussion, and conceptualization.

Category 4.40. Consideration of teachers' needs

4.41. Developers manifest awareness for the need for special training in order to teach the program, e.g.: The materials include background information in the subject matter domain.
4.42. Possible difficulties in teaching the materials are anticipated, e.g.: It is pointed out that certain misconceptions of students may interfere with the learning process.
4.43. The teachers' guide deals with interpersonal relationships (teacher-student; teacher-parent, etc.), i.e.: Teachers are advised to relate to students as partners in learning.
4.44. The teachers' guide reflects consideration of teachers' opinions and attitudes, e.g.: Teachers are advised to omit certain parts of a biology curriculum if they are uneasy about working with live organisms.

This analytic scheme allows teachers to uncover the nature of curriculum materials guided by a scheme which is based on certain frameworks, such as Bloom's taxonomy (1956) or Hunt's (1971, 1974) notions of learning style. It is important to stress that curriculum analysis provides teachers with an "anatomy" of the materials. The revealed map of curriculum characteristics has to be interpreted in the light of teachers' concerns and understanding of their classroom situation. Teachers may choose to analyze their curricula in any one or in a combination of dimensions, according to their interests and concerns. For instance, teachers whose main concern is the nature of the subject matter may find it useful to focus on this dimension. The Science Teachers' Association of Ontario published a Science Curriculum Policy Paper (1985) which describes the general characteristics of science content. They claim that

there is a wide discrepancy between the nature of science as it tends to be treated in school curricula and as it is described in the philosophy of science and in the science education literature on the nature of science . . . When philosophers of science and science educators refer to the nature of science they are thinking as much of the process of research and inquiry as they are of the products of that inquiry . . . The science curriculum ought to conceptualize and educate students in this dual understanding of the nature of science and not merely in terms of its products of knowledge. (*A Rationale for Quality Science Education*, p. 14)

Teachers who share these concerns may find that the analysis of the "subject matter" dimension in curriculum materials in science may lead to some implications for teaching and may yield changes and transformations in the materials they use.

Teachers whose main concerns are related to societal issues may tend to focus on the "milieu" dimension. The policy paper mentioned above argues that science curricula should be required to deal with a selected number of "science and society" issues, such as the manipulation of genetic characteristics. Teachers may decide on the proper priorities in teaching about such issues on the basis of their interpretation of the curriculum potential embedded in the materials they use.

Several teacher concerns related to curriculum matters were discussed in Chapter 3. One of the major concerns is the adaptability of materials to divergent student populations. Therefore, the "learner" dimension is considered very important for curriculum analysis. Teachers may decide that the materials do not offer opportunities for student development in certain areas. These insights may lead to a variety of nonlaboratory methods, such as simulation and role-playing, that will provide students with opportunities to develop their ability to think about scientific issues.

A full analysis may disclose a complex network of curriculum features. Conclusions may then be reached about the appropriateness of these features and their perceived potential for teaching.

You may try to use this instrument for analyzing your own curriculum materials. You may find the worksheet format in the appendix helpful for your analysis.

THE MATCHING WHEEL

In Chapter 5 we discussed the distinction between internal and external frames of reference. A simple instrument, the matching wheel (Ben-Peretz and Lifmann 1978), may serve curriculum interpretation in both the internal and external mode (see Figure 4).

THE MATCHING WHEEL

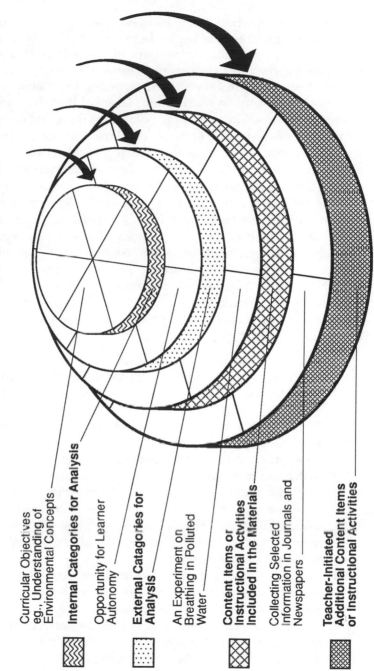

Curricular Objectives
eg., Understanding of
Environmental Concepts

Internal Categories for Analysis

Opportunity for Learner
Autonomy

**External Catagories for
Analysis**

An Experiment on
Breathing in Polluted
Water

**Content Items or
Instructional Activities
Included in the Materials**

Collecting Selected
Information in Journals and
Newspapers

**Teacher-Initiated
Additional Content Items
or Instructional Activities**

The matching wheel has to be viewed as a graphic representation of the matching principle underlying this instrument for
curriculum interpretation. It consists of several divided layers
which are attached to an underlying platform by a pin at the axis
of the wheel. This pin allows the user to devise different combinations of sections of layers. The four layers of the wheel are designated as follows. The two uppermost layers represent categories
for analysis and interpretation. On one layer the curriculum analyst notes internal categories, such as objectives determined by the
developers, for instance, "understanding of environmental concepts." On the second layer of the wheel external categories of
analysis are noted, stemming from frames of reference which are
not part of the developers' platforms, for instance, "opportunity
for learner autonomy." Sections of the two lower layers represent
components of curriculum materials, content items, or activities
that are part of the materials, such as "an experiment on breathing
in polluted water." On layer 4, one notes teacher-initiated, additional items or activities, such as "collecting related information in
journals and newspapers." The process of analysis and interpretation proceeds as follows:

1. Choose a chapter or section from a set of curriculum
   materials, such as a student textbook. Number the passages of text or other curriculum items, illustrations,
   home assignments, and so forth.
2. Decide which internal and which external categories
   you will use for your analysis, and note these on the
   appropriate sections of the matching wheel.
3. Match the numbered parts of the curriculum materials
   with the appropriate sections of categories. For instance, an experiment on breathing in water could be
   matched with the objective "understanding of environmental concepts," as well as with the category "opportunity for learner autonomy."
4. Devise additional items of content or activities that
   match with your chosen internal and external categories of analysis. Note these on layer 4.
5. By trying out different possible matches between categories and curricular items, one explores the educational potential embodied in these items.

6. By suggesting additional items and activities, one extends the possible uses of existing curriculum materials.

The matching wheel is based on the following principles:

1. The principle of matching. Portions and elements of materials are matched with diverse opportunities for learning, some intended and some unintended by curriculum developers.
2. The principle of diversity. Diversity expresses itself in the different categories which may be used for matching and in the suggestions for learning activities.
3. The principle of teacher autonomy. Teachers are expected to treat sets of curriculum materials as flexibly as possible, according to their own insights into their educational potential.

The matching wheel may be used to quantify one's findings. For instance, teachers searching for expressions of humor or human interest in curriculum materials may count all matching items and arrive at a quantitative portrayal of curriculum materials. Curriculum interpretation based on the matching of analytic categories with concrete components of the materials may be very helpful in the preactive phase of teaching, the planning of lessons.

Group discussions based on individual attempts of curriculum interpretations through the use of the matching wheel provide opportunities for sharing ideas and for clarifying their educational implications. Teachers who use this instrument may be able to suggest and elaborate a wide range of learning experiences originating in a given set of curriculum materials.

You may wish to try to use the "matching wheel" for different purposes, for instance, for planning your lessons based on a given set of curriculum materials. You may also use the "matching wheel" to compare different materials in order to choose those which are most appropriate for your teaching situations. You may try to involve your students in analyzing the materials, helping them become aware of their nature.

CONCLUDING COMMENTS

Four different instruments for curriculum analysis and interpretation were presented in this chapter. All instruments are designed for a more active role of teachers regarding curriculum. Analysis of curriculum materials is considered essential for interpreting their possible meaning in different educational situations. Because of the divergent nature of the instruments, they may promote teachers' motivation to try new ways in curriculum implementation. The various instruments are not subject matter bound, and therefore it is possible to adapt them according to teachers' interests and areas of teaching. Although the four instruments are described in detail, they can and should be adapted to varying circumstances. Additional instruments may be devised by teachers.

This leads us to one of teachers' crucial concerns, the issue of the balance between coverage of a given curricular content and the individual choices of teachers and students. One possible solution to this dilemma is that teachers decide on certain ideas, concepts, and knowledge items which will form a core curriculum. Beyond this core teachers will continue to explore other options and choices which they consider appropriate for their teaching circumstances. It is contended that the analysis and interpretation of curriculum materials are a prerequisite for deciding about defensible components of the core curriculum.

RECOMMENDED ADDITIONAL READINGS

If you are interested in Kelly's theory of personal constructs, you may find the following writings interesting:

Kelly, G. A. (1955): *The Psychology of Personal Constructs*, New York, Norton.

Adams-Webber, S. R. (1979): *Personal Construct Theory, Concepts and Applications*, New York, John Wiley and Sons.

Pope, M. L., and Keen, T. R. (1981): *Personal Construct Psychology and Education*, London, Academic Press.

A glimpse of constructs used by teachers in relation to curriculum materials is provided by *Beyond Surface Curriculum* by A. M. Bussis, E. A. Chittenden, and M. Amarel (1976), Boulder, Col., Westview Press.

7

Implications for Teacher Education and Staff Development

*"Anything is possible if you don't know
what you're talking about"*
A. Block, Murphy's Law Book Two, *1985, p. 51*

Teachers are often admonished to be autonomous in their teaching and to act as professional decision makers in all areas of teaching, including their lesson planning. Loewenberg-Ball and Feiman-Nemser (1988) established that different teacher education programs may communicate a common message about textbooks and teachers' guides, that they should be used only as resources for flexible planning. Teachers are not supposed to be "text bound." This claim may be based on unrealistic expectations, especially as far as beginning teachers are concerned. The previous chapters emphasized teachers' role as curriculum interpreters who base their lesson planning on their insights into the educational potential embodied in curriculum materials. Without such insights teachers may remain "text bound," using textbooks or teacher guides because they "are there," without attempting adaptation or enrichment of existing materials. It may not be realistic to expect teachers to develop their own curriculum materials. On the other hand, standard textbooks and regulated guidebooks may not be appropriate for specific educational situations. This is not necessarily a question of curricular deficiencies, although they do exist. It has been stated, for instance, that "the textbook programs that dominate U.S.–elementary school classrooms have been criticized for their representation of content; their implicit assumptions about teachers, students, teaching, and learning; and their social and cultural biases" (Loewenberg-Ball and Feiman-Nemser 1988, p. 401). The need to elaborate and change curriculum materials is a part of everyday school life that is meant to enhance the learning opportunities offered to students. Teachers' engagement in this process of elaboration and change may be considered a cardinal component of their professional activities. In order to be able to accomplish these activities, it is contended that the following abilities are required:

- Analysis and interpretation of different kinds of curriculum materials
- Selection, sequencing, and transformation of curricular components according to perceived needs arising in specific educational situations
- Creation of additional curriculum units beyond those specified in a given set of curriculum materials

The question arises of how to incorporate these abilities in teacher education programs. Educating student-teachers for sensitive and sophisticated curriculum interpretation may be a problematic goal for preservice teacher education: "Using materials thoughtfully requires an understanding of the meaning and possible consequences of the way they are designed and what they include" (Loewenberg-Ball and Feiman-Nemser 1988, p. 420). Without significant experience in classroom teaching, teachers may find it difficult to anticipate possible consequences of curriculum uses. It probably takes years of experience to acquire the kind of "curriculum knowledge" and "pedagogical content knowledge" that Shulman (1987) counts among the important categories of the knowledge base for teaching. Therefore, it seems that staff development for teachers who have already gained teaching experience plays an important role in helping teachers with curricular issues. Preservice teacher education, on the other hand, may be conceived as laying the necessary foundations for the future development and growth of the abilities needed for reflective, problem-solving-oriented, and creative curriculum use.[14]

COMPONENTS OF TEACHER EDUCATION PROGRAMS FOR CURRICULUM USE

Teacher education programs providing the necessary foundation for reflective involvement in curriculum issues and for curriculum literacy of teachers would include the following elements:

- Awareness of "choice points" in curriculum development

- Experiences with a variety of approaches and instruments for curriculum analysis and interpretations
- Participation in curriculum development exercises
- Reflection on curriculum implementation studies
- Cooperation and collaboration with peers

We shall deal with each of these points separately.

Choice Points in Curriculum Development

Curriculum developers make deliberate choices about subject matter, learners, and anticipated teaching acts. They decide on curriculum format, content, scope, and sequence. These decisions may be viewed as occurring at "choice points." According to Connelly (1972), "a choice point refers to a philosophical, psychological, sociological or methodological issue that underlies particular curriculum development" (p. 172). Developers decide which of a number of possible alternatives to adopt at each choice point. Examples of questions that developers may ask themselves at curricular decision points are as follows: What information should be included in the materials? What aspects of knowledge should be emphasized? What meaningful societal or personal issues can be dealt with by means of the specific content? Decisions related to such questions express the educational potential of the curriculum as identified by the developers.

Awareness of these choice points and sufficient pedagogical knowledge to grasp the meaning and possible consequences of adopting the chosen alternatives are important for teachers, whether they use externally developed materials or develop their own curriculum. Preservice teacher education programs may aid students in gaining insights into the nature of the development process itself, including the notion of choice points.

How can the understanding of choice points be incorporated in teacher education programs? One way of doing this is by reflecting about the role that different theories may play in curricular decision making. For instance, student-teachers or teachers in staff development programs could consider the possible impact of behaviorism on the nature of curriculum materials. They could ask themselves how developers who choose to be guided by behaviorist learning theory would structure their materials. Another question to treat would be how Piagetian cognitive theory could shape curriculum materials.

The issue of choice points may be approached in another way, namely, through a careful reading of curriculum materials. For instance, student-teachers and teachers could ask questions regarding the specific content chosen for inclusion in a set of curriculum materials and list other alternatives and their possible consequences for students. Through the examination of curriculum materials student-teachers and teachers may become sensitive to choice points in curriculum development.

"Reading" of curriculum materials was discussed in previous chapters and will be mentioned only briefly in the next section.

Curriculum Analysis and Interpretation

One of the strategies for fostering insights into curricular processes is through structured analysis of syllabi and curriculum materials. By learning to analyze syllabi, student-teachers may become sensitive to the kind of choices adopted by curriculum developers and textbook writers. Syllabus analysis was discussed and exemplified in previous chapters.

The combination of learning about theoretical choice points and actively participating in curriculum analysis may provide a basis for curriculum literacy. Curriculum literacy is deemed necessary for freeing teachers from the bondage of textbooks and guidelines. Knowledge about the nature of curricular decisions and the great variability of possible curricular solutions is part of the "inside story" of curriculum making and provides the first step toward teachers' curricular autonomy.

Curriculum analysis and interpretation may be extended beyond the uncovering of choice points. By learning about a variety of analytic instruments and by experimenting with their uses for different purposes, student-teachers may acquire interpretative skills and feelings for the nuances of curriculum materials. The aim of curriculum analysis is not only to gain insights into the deliberations and choices of developers, but also to reveal new and unexpected uses of the materials in the daily practice of teachers. Student-teachers and teachers who learn to use a variety of instruments in order to uncover the educational potential embodied in materials may gain insights into their complexity and richness. It is important to learn to apply different instruments in curriculum analysis because any one may be limited in the kinds of insights it provides.

Learning about curricular choice points and about the manifold educational possibilities which may be embedded in curriculum materials is considered a prerequisite for active experiences in curriculum development.

Participation in Curriculum Development

Teacher education programs are appropriate contexts for participating in curriculum development experiences in unthreatening circumstances without being pressed to use the products in one's own classrooms. Participation in curriculum development provides student-teachers or teachers with opportunities for experiencing decision making at the various crossroads of development: choice of content, choice of instructional strategies, and decisions about scope and sequence. An example of incorporating curriculum development experience in teacher education is the graduate studies practicum described by Connelly and Ben-Peretz (1980). In one instance, graduate studies practicum students worked for a full year with a geography curriculum committee. Participants learned about the resolution of curricular problems and the intricacies of the process of development.

Actual experiences in curriculum development, as exemplified in Chapter 1, combined with learning about different theoretical approaches to curriculum development and implementation, provide student-teachers or teachers with an insider's view of curriculum. An insider's view of curriculum development may sharpen teachers' faculties for dealing with ready-made curriculum materials in their everyday professional lives.

You may try to become involved in such experiences in your own school setting.

Reflection on Curriculum Implementation Studies

It has already been stated that curriculum use constitutes part of teacher's daily practice. In order to expand teachers' curricular horizons, it seems advisable to engage them in reflection on studies of curriculum implementation. Through the examination of such investigations, such as Reid's and Walker's (1975) case studies in curriculum change, teachers would gain insights into the problems that arise in the implementation process.

One of these case studies focuses on ways of handling innovation in the classroom (Hamilton 1975). This study shows that teachers are worried about interference effects which may result from a mismatch between curricular innovations and the learning milieu. The case study reminds us that teachers do not function as curriculum technicians but as selective agents who act as critical mediators in implementation and who may introduce major modifications in their curriculum.

These insights may help teachers who experience failures in using curriculum materials even though they are convinced of the materials' inherent value to their students. Sensitivity to the many factors which are involved in curriculum use may be helpful in clarifying reasons for failures and may indicate different modes of implementation.

Cooperation and Collaboration

Teachers' anticipated encounters with curriculum material require cooperative and collaborative skills. Such skills may be fostered by special strategies of instruction in teacher education programs. In the reform of teacher education, emphasis has to be given to developing teachers' ability to cooperate with pupils, colleagues, and community groups. Taylor (1978) notes that these tendencies are reflected in the emphasis on group activities that are designed to promote personal growth through interaction in a supporting environment. These kinds of activities may well serve teachers in their future involvement in curricular activities, such as teamwork in adapting curriculum to local needs. It may be argued that participation in joint curriculum analysis activities, small development projects, and group discussions related to curriculum choice points during teacher education may contribute to the development of the cooperative skills which are required for a wide range of teachers' professional functions.

One intriguing teaching approach aiming at improving interpretative abilities through group interaction was suggested by Abercrombie (1965). Abercrombie taught medical students to interpret X-ray pictures using small group discussion techniques. "In the discussion technique of teaching, the student learns by comparing his observation with those of ten or so of his peers. He compares not only the results, but how the results were arrived at" (Abercrombie 1965, p. 17). Group discussions are not a new instructional strategy; what is new in Abercrombie's attempt is her use of this strategy to enhance interpretative skills of phenomena which may appear to the layman to have only one possible interpretation. Abercrombie tries to make her students understand the selective and interpretative nature of perception, and shows how the information that a person gets from a specified part of the outer world depends on the context, on the total situation, and on his or her past experiences. She stresses the important role that human relationships play in perception and interpretation and states that during the discussions the students were mutually testing and modifying the schemata they used for interpretation. As a result of reorganizing their store of experience in this way, they enhanced their abilities to make more valid interpretations.

Group discussions of student-teachers relating to their analysis of curriculum materials would serve the same purposes mentioned by Abercrombie. Students would come to understand their own ways of perceiving materials, and through their interaction with others, would be able to arrive at more elaborate and valid interpretations. An additional reason for conducting curriculum analysis and interpretation as group activities is that through these experiences student-teachers and teachers may form dispositions toward the cooperative planning of their courses.

Constructive and productive group interactions require special skills. Reid (1988) suggests that specific techniques are needed to prepare teachers for their role in solving practical problems of the curriculum through school-based deliberations in groups. Some of these specific techniques may be incorporated in teacher education programs. What is the nature of such techniques? According to Reid, teachers need to have access to a range of methods and procedures answering a number of purposes: the gathering and readying of a group, the management of personal relations in a group, the provision of information to a group, the allocation of tasks in a group, and so on. Sustained activites of curriculum planning, conducted in groups of teachers and reflected upon continuously, are considered to be one of the main features of teacher education for the flexible use and creation of curriculum materials. Curricular deliberation carried out under these circumstances is a process through which the nature of a problem is exposed and varied solutions are being devised. Each step is contingent on preceding steps: at each moment method and subject matter interact. Most important, study and deliberation groups emphasize the role of *teachers as learners* who continuously enhance their knowledge and enrich their understanding of the nature of curriculum materials which have to be adapted to the diverse interests and abilities of learners. The very notion of curriculum potential bears the inherent message of continuous learning. Each time teachers reinterpret the curriculum materials they use, they may discover new angles and unintended possibilities. Relearning the curriculum is a process which benefits greatly from interaction with colleagues through the exchange of ideas and experiences. In the kind of group activities mentioned here, teachers may share their pedagogical content knowledge, thus extending the knowledge base of each.

You may wish to set up a special staff development program in your school focusing on the kind of group activities described above.

So far we have discussed some elements of teacher education programs for curriculum literacy and for the flexible use of curriculum materials. What settings of teacher education programs would be appropriate for these kinds of activities?

SETTINGS AND ORGANIZATIONAL FRAMEWORKS

It has been argued that student-teachers may find it difficult to perceive the educational meanings of curriculum materials. Because of their lack of practical experience in the classroom, they would benefit from the shared "wisdom of practice" of experienced teachers. Therefore it is contended that joint settings bringing together novices and expert teachers to interact in curriculum interpretation and planning would be most productive. Problems and issues raised by student-teachers or beginning practitioners would allow veteran teachers to question some of their own accustomed ways of dealing with matters of curriculum. On the other hand, the curricular wisdom of experienced practitioners could help novices in their initial attempts to deal with pressing concerns, such as the dilemma of content coverage versus in-depth study of selected topics.

Joint settings dealing with curricular issues could become part of preservice teacher education programs. The practicum component of programs offers many opportunities for organizing such settings. The induction phase of beginning teachers is another appropriate period for engaging jointly in gaining curriculum literacy.

Special organizational frameworks may be set up for this purpose. Goodlad (1984) recommends the creation of special centers designed to attend to research and development in school curricula. Such centers, embracing specific domains of knowledge or geared to special age groups or to special needs of students, would be appropriate as sites for joint settings of student-teachers and teachers. In these centers teachers could participate in the development of new curricula or in the creative reorganizing of existing materials. These materials could then be used in the classes of participating teachers. Follow-up reflection would provide the necessary feedback for the improvement of curricular skills.

CONCLUDING COMMENTS

Pre- and in-service teacher education programs play a major role in providing opportunities for reflecting on one's own practice and for extending professional abilities. Learning to teach is a continuous process which goes on through all the years of practicing teaching. Freeing teachers from the tyranny of curricular texts may be viewed as an evolutionary process which starts with attempts at using these texts after carefully interpreting and discovering their educational potential. School-based curriculum development may be viewed as constituting the highest level of this process. School-based curriculum development means that decisions about the nature of the curriculum that should be available to students in any school are made by the staff of that school. School-based curriculum development may also mean the attempts of individual teachers to prepare curriculum materials, such as texts or worksheets, for their own classes. In each case, decisions have to be made about goals, content, resources, and specific learning strategies. Therefore, school based curriculum development implies that teachers accept greater responsibility for curriculum decision making. Reid claims that "this in turn implies that schools and teachers need to have resources and abilities for decision making over and above these that they customarily employ" (Reid 1988, p. 110). According to Reid (1988), the habits of curriculum deliberation are to be seen as "instances of the exercise of virtues, and therefore have to be learned through doing" (p. 112). Cooperative efforts of curriculum interpretation and planning in specially designed joint settings are conceived as opportunities for learning through doing.

Loewenberg-Ball and Feiman-Nemser (1988) suggest that ready-made curricular materials may provide "instructional scaffolding" (Vigotsky 1978) for novice teachers who learn to teach. Instructional scaffolding is perceived as a process which supports the involvement of novices in performing their tasks. Gradually student-teachers, interacting with experienced colleagues, may acquire expertise in using materials wisely and autonomously.

In the theoretical realm, knowledge of curriculum terminology, curricular concepts, and processes would give student-teachers and teachers a sense of some of the professional aspects of teaching, thus promoting an awareness of "a shared body of specialized knowledge" (Lortie 1975, p. 80). In the practical realm, student-teachers and teachers who are involved in curriculum interpretation exercises and in instructional planning based on their personal interpretations may gain confidence in their ability to use curriculum materials. It seems important, however, to note that mastery of the relevant subject matter area is crucial for exercising this ability.

Throughout this book the issue of teachers' concerns relating to curriculum was raised. Several concerns were mentioned specifically:

1. Concerns related to the subject matter content of curriculum materials
2. Concerns related to the adaptability of materials to divergent student audiences
3. Concerns related to the dilemma between broad coverage of themes versus in-depth learning of chosen topics
4. Concern about lack of the curricular knowledge which is required for the use and creation of curriculum materials
5. Concerns about autonomy in decision making related to curriculum

It is our claim that curriculum literacy gained through some of the recommended strategies would help teachers cope with these concerns.

Teachers may deal with their concern regarding the content of curriculum materials and its adaptability to their students by carefully analyzing the curriculum, clarifying the nature of the subject matter that is included in the text. Curriculum analysis may yield important insights into the validity of the content and its relevance to specific student populations. Using internal schemes of analysis may enable teachers to deal with their concern about curriculum coverage. Identifying the main characteristics of any mandated curriculum allows teachers to create a core curriculum while still giving them freedom to plan additional learning experiences. In-depth understanding of the curriculum texts provides a basis for choosing appropriately and for introducing necessary transformations in the materials.

Teachers' involvement in curriculum interpretation employing the conceptual framework and the instruments presented in this book may contribute to the growth of their curricular knowledge. The ultimate goal of this endeavor is to liberate teachers from the tyranny of the curriculum text so that they will become truly autonomous regarding their curriculum.

RECOMMENDED ADDITIONAL READINGS

Lee Shulman's article (1987): "Knowledge and teaching: Foundations of the new reform," *Harvard Educational Review* 57, 1: 1–22, provides a comprehensive framework for thinking about the knowledge base for teaching; it emphasizes the need for teachers' involvement in the transformation of texts for teaching purposes.

Teachers' Professional Learning, edited by J. Calderhead (1988), London, Falmer Press, treats various aspects of teachers' professional growth. Especially relevant to the ideas of this book are the following chapters:

- Russell, T., "From pre-service teacher education to first year of teaching: A theory of theory and practice" (pp. 13–34)
- McIntyre, D., "Designing a teacher education curriculum from research and theory on teacher knowledge" (pp. 97–114)
- Johnston, K., "Changing teachers' conceptions of teaching and learning" (pp. 169–195)
- Rudduck, J., "The ownership of change as a basis for teachers' professional learning (pp. 204–222)

John Haysom's (1985) book, *Inquiring into the Teaching Process: Towards Self-evaluation and Professional Development*, Toronto, OISE Press, treats various aspects of teaching and professional development from the perspective of practitioners.

Notes

1. Biology curricula and biology teachers serve as common examples throughout this book, although other subject matter areas are treated as well. The author's background in science education, especially in biology teaching, leads her to conduct research in this area. Moreover, many curricular innovations have been developed, implemented, and studied in the context of biology teaching. It is contended that the conceptual framework of this book and the analytic instruments are applicable to all subject matter areas.

2. In this context, *content orientation* refers to an emphasis on subject matter, on information, concepts, and principles. The main goals of a content-oriented curriculum are perceived to be acquisition of knowledge. *Process orientation* is conceived as pertaining to cognitive or interpersonal abilities or skills. The main goals of a process-oriented curriculum tend to be the acquisition of behaviors related to these abilities and skills.

3. *School-based curriculum development* refers to school autonomy exercised in the realm of decisions regarding the detailed contents to be taught, the ways of organizing and presenting the chosen themes, and the selection of appropriate materials and resources to be utilized in the school, including texts. See. M. Skilbeck (1987): "School-based curriculum development and central curriculum policies in England and Wales: A paradox in three acts," in N. Sabar, J. Rudduck, and W. Reid (eds.), *Partnership and Autonomy In School-based Curriculum Development*, USDE Papers in Education, University of Sheffield, pp. 16–27.

4. The "structure of knowledge" or "structure of the disciplines" approach to curriculum development had a powerful impact on curriculum development in the 1960s and early 1970s. These were the years in which large-scale efforts were made, especially in the United States, to reform and improve education through curriculum materials. Adopting this approach means that curricula in various disciplines, such as mathematics or history,

121

reflect the key concepts, principles, and methods of inquiry which characterize the discipline. The "structure of knowledge" approach was argued for in J. Bruner's book (1961): *The Process of Education*, Cambridge, Mass., Harvard University Press. Schwab (1964) discussed at length the nature of subject matter for schooling, and distinguished between the substantive and the syntactic structures of the disciplines in his essay, "Problems, topics and issues," in S. Elam, ed., *Education and the Structure of Knowledge*, Chicago, Rand McNally, pp. 4–47.

5. The research about the particular difficulties in the teaching of the Holocaust is vast. The two most accepted textbooks in Israel today are actually representing the two main aspects under discussion. One by I. Gutman and C. Schatzker (1983): *The Holocaust and Its Significance*, Jerusalem, Zalman Shazar Centre, stays more within the cognitive realm of the historical processes which led to the Holocaust. The other book, written by A. Carmon (1981), *Holocaust*, Jerusalem, Ministry of Education and Culture, Centre for Curriculum Development, stresses the aspects of teaching values and thus emphasizes a more affective approach.

6. "Change agents" in this context are teacher educators and members of the special support staff of teachers.

7. The term *curriculum potential* was used by Schwab (1973) with reference to the manifold ways in which curriculum developers may use scholarly writings, such as scientific papers, which serve as sources for the construction of curriculum materials. Schwab called this the process of "translation" of scholarly materials into curriculum materials. In this book the term *curriculum potential* refers to the manifold possible uses of existing curriculum materials by teachers. The materials are conceived as sources for new, second-level interpretations (Ben-Peretz, M. (1975): "The concept of curriculum potential," *Curriculum Theory Network* 5, 2:151–159).

8. Several authors have discussed the 'hidden curriculum'. Jane Martin (1976) explored definitions of this concept and examined various ways of dealing with the hidden curriculum, once it has been uncovered. Martin suggests that consciousness raising with respect to hidden curricula is essential for overcoming their undesirable influences. Gordon (1988) has written extensively on the nature of the hidden curriculum. Drawing on the writings of

Ricoeur and Geertz (among them Ricoeur 1974, 1981, and Geertz 1973), he examines the notion of education as text. Gordon proposes the hypothesis that education as a text, read not only by students but by all members of society, becomes a text about society's myths and sacred beliefs.

9. The notion of pedagogical content knowledge, the blending of content and pedagogy, is part of Shulman's (1987) conception of the knowledge base of teaching. Shulman differentiates between the following categories of teacher knowledge: content knowledge, general pedagogical knowledge, curriculum knowledge, pedagogical content knowledge, knowledge of learners, knowledge of educational contexts, and knowledge of educational ends. According to Shulman, "pedagogical content knowledge is the category most likely to distinguish the understanding of the content specialist from that of the pedagogue" (p. 8).

10. The subjective/objective distinction has obtained much attention in philosophical writings. Buchman (1989) states that objectivity is "an ideal that animates much human effort at comprehension, inside and outside of science" (p. 11). She claims that "the attraction of this ideal derives from an assumption that things are what they are from no particular perspective, and that de-centering moves us closer toward truth and justice" (p. 11). Buchman quotes Francis Bacon, who said that "it is a poor center of a man's action, himself" and goes on to say that "from this point of view, the subject is a source of distortion and must itself be set aside" (Buchman, p. 11).

Erickson (1986) states that "the assumption of uniformity of nature, and of mechanical, chemical, and biological metaphors for causal relations among individual entities is taken over from the natural sciences in positivist social and behavioral sciences" (p. 126). According to Erickson, the interpretive perspective asserts that humans create meaningful interpretations of the world around them. The interpretive approach calls for identification of the subjective meanings and interpretations of humans in different situations. Teachers' subjective interpretations of curriculum materials focus on personally assigned meanings. Objective interpretations set the teacher aside and focus on categories of analysis which come from outside sources.

11. Kelly's theory of personal constructs has stimulated much research in different areas of inquiry. The following are some examples. A special issue of *Interchange*, Vol. 13, No. 4 (1982), was devoted to the theme of personal constructs in education. Pope and Keen (1981) suggested that Kelly's approach had policy implications for curriculum design and pedagogical practice. Ben-Peretz (1984) analyzed the appropriateness of Kelly's theory for investigating teachers' thinking. Brown (1984) argues that personal construct theory may be useful for school administrators in their search for developing their own professional thinking. Hunt's book, *Beginning with Ourselves* (1987), is based on his use of Kelly's Rep test to reveal the implicit educational theories of hundreds of practitioners.

12. Connelly and Clandinin (1985) developed the idea of personal practical knowledge. They state that personal practical knowledge is "a moral affective and aesthetic way of knowing life's educational situations" (Connelly and Clandinin 1988, p. 59). They have developed a "language of practice" for teaching about educational situations. Some of the central concepts in this language are rules, practical principles, and images—proposed by Elbaz (1983). Other cardinal concepts are rhythms, metaphors, personal philosophy, and narrative unity, developed by Connelly and Clandinin who describe this language of educational practice in their chapter "Your Personal Practical Knowledge," (1988, pp. 59–78). An in-depth analysis of the notion of image is provided by Jean Clandinin in her book *Classroom Practice: Teacher Images in Action* (1986). The idea of personal practical knowledge constitutes a conceptual framework for many empirical studies of educational situations.

13. Several schemes of curriculum analysis have been developed based on different frameworks and different sets of categories for analysis. Eash (1971–1972), for instance, based his scheme of analysis on the Tylerian model of curriculum development. The categories for analysis in this scheme are objectives, organization of materials, methodology, and evaluation. The scheme proposed by Eash fulfills a normative function, setting a standard for judging curriculum materials. The analyst is asked to grade the materials on a continuum from very high to very low in all categories of analysis.

Eraut et al. (1975), on the other hand, do not determine standards for evaluating the analyzed materials. Their scheme presents varied views of the materials and leaves it to the analyst to assess their worth based on the insight gained through the analysis. Roberts and Russell (1975) propose a process for translating theoretical perspectives into analytical schemes. Their position is that theoretical perspectives have to be developed into structures that may serve the systematic analysis of educational phenomena, including curriculum materials.

14. Both student-teachers and experienced teachers may find it difficult to be flexible in their interpretations of curriculum materials. Student-teachers lack classroom experiences that might be a stimulus for uncovering curriculum potential in the text. Experienced teachers may have well-established routines of using curricular texts and may find it difficult to introduce changes. Group activities of curriculum interpretation using a variety of approaches may be an incentive for novel ways of using curriculum materials. Individual as well as group reflection on these novel uses is an important component of this process.

References

Abercrombie, M. L. J. (1965): *The Anatomy of Judgement: An Investigation into the Processes of Perception and Reasoning*, London, Hutchinson.

Adams-Webber, S. R. (1979): *Personal Construct Theory, Concepts and Applications*, New York, John Wiley and Sons.

Adar, L., and Fox, S. (1978): *Analysis of the Content and Use of a History Curriculum*, Jerusalem, School of Education, Hebrew University.

Ariav, T. (1989): "Curriculum analysis," in T. Husen and T. N. Postlewaith (eds.), *The International Encyclopedia of Education*, Supplementary Volumes, Oxford, Pergamon.

Atkins, J. M. (1970): "Behavioral objectives in curriculum design: A cautionary note," in J. R. Martin (ed.), *Readings in the Philosophy of Education: A Study of Curriculum*, Boston, Allyn and Bacon, pp. 32–38.

Bannister, D. (1970): *Perspectives in Personal Construct Theory*, Bexley, Kent.

Barnes, D. (1976): *From Communication to Curriculum*, London, Penguin.

Ben-Peretz, M. (1975): "The concept of curriculum potential," *Curriculum Theory Network* 5, 2: 151–159.

———— (1977): "Analysis and comparison of some high school biology curricula in Israel: Theoretical and practical considerations in the process of curriculum development," doctoral thesis, Hebrew University, Jerusalem.

———— (1980a): "Teachers' role in curriculum development: An alternative approach," *Canadian Journal of Education* 5, 2: 52–62.

———— (1980b): "Matriculation examinations and the school curriculum," *Studies in Education* 25: 37–46.

Ben-Peretz, M. (1981): "Curriculum analysis as a tool in evaluation," in A. Lewy and D. Nevo (eds.), *Evaluation Roles in Education*, New York, Gordon and Breach.

——— (1984): "Kelly's theory of personal constructs as a paradigm for investigating teacher thinking," in R. Halkes and I. K. Olson (eds.), *Teacher Thinking*, Lisse, Swets and Zeitlinger, pp. 103–111.

Ben-Peretz, M., Carre, C., and Sutton, C. (1977): "The development of teachers' competencies in generating curriculum potential," *Studies in Education* 17: 89–100.

Ben-Peretz, M., Katz, S., and Silberstein, M. (1982): "Curriculum interpretation and its place in teacher education programs," *Interchange* 13, 4: 47–55.

Ben-Peretz, M., and Kremer, L. (1979): "Curriculum implementation and the nature of curriculum materials," *Journal of Curriculum Studies* 11, 3: 247–255.

Ben-Peretz, M., and Lifmann, M. (1978): "Procedures and instruments for curriculum interpretation." Jerusalem, Ministry of Education and Culture.

Ben-Peretz, M., and Silberstein, M. (1982): "A curriculum development case study in biology: Two levels of interpretation," *European Journal of Science Education* 4,4: 377–389.

Ben-Peretz, M., and Tamir, P. (1981): "What teachers want to know about curriculum materials," *Journal of Curriculum Studies* 13, 1:45–54.

Berman, P., and McLaughlin, M. W. (1977): *Federal Programs Supporting Educational Change*, Vol. VII: *Factors Affecting Implementation and Continuation*, prepared for the U.S. Office of Education Department of Health, Education and Welfare, P-1578/7-HEW, Rand Corporation, Santa Monica, Calif.

Bloch, A. (1985): *Murphy's Law Book Two*, London, Methuen.

Bloom, B. S. (ed.) (1956): *Taxonomy of Educational Objectives*, Handbook I: *Cognitive Domain*, New York, David McKay.

Borko, H., Livingston, C., McCalleb, J., and Mauro, L. (1988): "Student-teachers planning and post-lesson reflection," in

J. Calderhead (ed.), *Teachers Professional Learning*, London, New York, Philadelphia, Falmer Press.

Bridgham, K. E. (1971): "Comments on some thoughts on science curriculum development," in E. W. Eisner (ed.), *Confronting Curriculum Reform*, Boston, Little Brown.

Brown, A. F. (1984): "How to change what teachers think about teachers: Affirmative action in promotion decisions" in R. Halkes and T. K. Olson (eds.), *Teacher Thinking: A New Perspective on Persisting Problems in Education* Lisse, Swets and Zeitlinger.

Brown, A. F., and Ritchie T. J. (1982): Issue theme: "Personal Constructs," *Interchange* 13, 4.

Bruner, J. (1961): *The Process of Education*, Cambridge, Mass., Harvard University Press.

Buchman, M. (1989): "The careful vision: How practical is contemplation in teaching?" Issue Paper 89-1, East Lansing, Michigan State University, National Center for Research on Teacher Education.

Bussis, A. M., Chittenden, E. A., and Amarel, M. (1976): *Beyond Surface Curriculum*, Boulder, Col., Westview Press.

Butt, R., Raymond, M. D., and Ray, J. (1986): "Personal, practical and prescriptive influences on teacher's thoughts and actions," paper presented at the 1986 conference of the International Study Association on Teacher Thinking (ISATT), Leuven, Belgium, October 14–17.

Carmon, A. (1981): *Holocaust*, Jerusalem, Ministry of Education and Culture, Centre for Curriculum Development.

Clandinin, D. J. (1986): *Classroom Practice: Teacher Images in Action*, Barcombe Lewes, Falmer Press.

Clark, C. M., and Yinger, R. J. (1977): "Research on teacher thinking," *Curriculum Inquiry* 7, 2: 279–304.

——— (1979): "Three studies of teacher planning," Research series No. 55, East Lansing, Michigan State University.

Connelly, F. M. (1972): "The functions of curriculum development," *Interchange* 2,3: 161–177.

Connelly, F. M., and Ben-Peretz, M. (1980): "Teachers' roles in the using and doing of research and curriculum development," *Journal of Curriculum Studies* 12, 2: 95–107.

Connelly, F. M., Ben-Peretz, M., and Enns, R. J. (1978): "Assessing the compatability of curriculum policy and school programs with external testing," *The Crucible* 9, 6: 4–10.

Connelly, F. M., and Clandinin, D. J. (1985): "Personal practical knowledge and the modes of knowing: Relevance for teaching and learning," in *Learning and Teaching: The Ways of Knowing*, NSSE Yearbook, 84/2, University of Chicago Press, pp. 174–98.

———— (1988): *Teachers as Curriculum Planners: Narratives of Experience*, New York, Teachers College Press, and Toronto, OISE Press.

Connelly, F. M., and Elbaz, F. (1980): "Conceptual bases for curriculum thought: A teacher's perspective," in A. W. Foshay (ed.), *Considered Action for Curriculum Improvement*, Washington, D.C., Association for Supervision and Curriculum Development, pp. 95–119.

Dickson, P. (1978): *The Official Rules*, New York, Dela Corte Press.

Eash, M. H. (1971–1972): "Developing an instrument for assessing instructional materials," *Curriculum Theory Network* 8, 9: 59–69.

Eisner, E. W. (1979): *The Educational Imagination: On the Design and Evaluation of School Programs*, New York, Macmillan.

Elbaz, F. (1983): *Teacher Thinking: A Study of Practical Knowledge*, London, Croom Helm.

Eraut, M., Goad, L., and Smith, G. (1975): "The analysis of curriculum materials," Educational Area, Occasional papers 2, Brighton, University of Sussex.

Erickson, F. (1986): "Qualitative methods in research on teaching," in M. C. Wittrock (ed.), *Handbook for Research on Teaching*, 3rd Edition, New York, Macmillan.

Flesh, R. F. (1951): *How to Test Readability*, New York, Harper and Row.

Flinders, D. J., Noddings, N., and Thornton, S. T. (1986): "The null curriculum: Its theoretical basis and practical implications," *Curriculum Inquiry* 16, 1: 33–42.

Fox, S. (1972): "A practical image of the 'practical'," *Curriculum Theory Network* 10: 45–57.

Fullan, M. (1982): *The Meaning of Educational Change*, Toronto, OISE Press.

Fullan, M., and Pomfret, A. (1977): "Research on curriculum and instruction implementation," *Review of Educational Research* 47, 1: 335–397.

Geertz, C. (1973): *The Interpretation of Cultures*, New York, Basic Books.

Goodlad, J. (1984): *A Place Called School*, New York, St. Louis, San Francisco, McGraw-Hill.

Gordon, D. (1982): "The concept of the hidden curriculum," *Journal of Philosophy of Education* 16, 2: 187–198.

────── (1984): "The image of science, technological consciousness and hidden curriculum," *Curriculum Inquiry* 14, 4: 367–400.

────── (1988): "Education as text: The varieties of educational hiddenness," *Curriculum Inquiry* 18, 4: 425–449.

Gudmunsdottir, S. (1988): "Curriculum stories: Four case studies of social studies teaching," paper presented at the biannual meeting of the International Study Association of Teacher Thinking (ISATT), Nottingham, September.

Gudmunsdottir, S., and Shulman, L. S. (1986): "Pedagogical content knowledge in social studies." Paper presented at the third conference on teacher thinking and professional action, ISATT meeting, Leuven; proceedings of the conference, Leuven University, Belgium.

Gutman, I., and Schatzker, C. (1983): *The Holocaust and Its Significance*, Jerusalem, Zalman Shazar Centre.

Halkes, R., and Olson, J. K. (eds.) (1984): *Teacher Thinking: A New Perspective on Persisting Problems in Education*, Lisse, Swets and Zeitlinger.

Hamilton, D. (1975): "Handling innovations in the classroom. Two Scottish examples," in W. A. Reid and D. F. Walker (eds.), *Case Studies in Curriculum Change*, London and Boston, Routledge and Kegan Paul, pp. 179–207.

Haysom, J. (1985): *Inquiring into the Teaching Process: Towards Self-evaluation and Professional Development*, Research in Education Series 12, Toronto, OISE Press.

Hunt, D. E. (1971): "Matching models in education: The coordination of teaching methods with student characteristics," Toronto, Ontario Institute for Studies in Education.

—— (1974): "Learning styles and teaching strategies," *Behavioral and Social Science Teacher* 2, 1: 22–34.

—— (1987): *Beginning with Ourselves: In Practice, Theory and Human Affairs*, Cambridge, Mass., Brookline Books, and Toronto, OISE Press.

Jackson, P. W. (1968): *Life in Classrooms*, New York, Holt, Rinehart and Winston.

—— (1986): *The Practice of Teaching*, New York and London, Teachers College Press.

Johnson, M. J. (1967): "Definition and models in curriculum theory," *Educational Theory* 17, 2: 127–140.

Johnston, K. (1988): "Changing teachers' conception of teaching and learning," in J. Calderhead (ed.), *Teachers' Professional Learning*, London, Falmer Press, pp. 169–185.

Kelly, G. A. (1955): *The Psychology of Personal Constructs*, New York, Norton.

Kennedy, K. J., and McDonald, G. (1986): "Designing curriculum materials for multicultural education. Lessons from an Australian Development Project," *Curriculum Inquiry* 16, 3: 311–326.

Kilbourn, B. (1974): "Identifying world views projected by science teaching materials. A case study using Pepper's world views hypothesis to analyze a biology textbook," doctoral thesis, University of Toronto.

Leithwood, K. A. (1976): *A Decision-oriented Strategy for Curriculum*

Implementation, Toronto, The Ontario Institute for Studies in Education.

Leithwood, K., and MacDonald, R. (1981): "Decisions given by teachers for their curriculum choices," *Canadian Journal of Education* 6, 2: 103–116.

Loewenberg-Ball, D., and Feiman-Nemser, S. (1988): "Using textbooks and teachers' guides: A dilemma for beginning teachers and teacher educators." *Curriculum Inquiry* 18, 4: 401–423.

Lortie, D. C. (1975): *Schoolteacher: A Sociological Study*, Chicago, University of Chicago Press.

McCutcheon, G. (1980): "How do elementary school teachers plan? The nature of planning and influences on it," *The Elementary School Journal* 81, 1: 4–23.

MacDonald, R. A., and Leithwood, K. A. (1982): "Toward an explanation of influences on teachers' curriculum decisions," in K. A. Leithwood (ed.), *Studies in Curriculum Decision Making*, Symposium Series 13, Toronto, OISE Press.

McIntyre, D. (1988): "Designing a teacher education curriculum from research and theory on teacher education," in J. Calderhead (ed.), *Teachers' Professional Learning*, London, Falmer Press, pp. 97–114.

McLaughlin, M., and Marsh, D. (1978): "Staff development and school change," *Teachers College Record* 80, 1: 69–94.

Martin, J. R. (1976): "What should we do with a hidden curriculum when we find one?" *Curriculum Inquiry* 6, 2: 135–151.

Meyer, H. L. (1972): "Das ungeloeste Deduktions problem in der Curriculumforschung," in H. L. Meyer (ed.), *Curriculum Revision—Moeglichzeiten und Grenzen*, Munich, Kosel Verlag.

Oliver, A. J. (1977): *Curriculum Improvement*, New York, Harper and Row.

Pepper, S. C. (1942): *World Hypothesis: A Study in Evidence*, Berkeley, University of California Press.

Peters, R. S. (1967): "What is an educational process?" in R. S. Peters (ed.), *The Concept of Education*, London, Routledge and Kegan Paul.

Peterson, P. L., Marx, R. W., and Clark, C. M. (1978): "Teacher planning, teacher behavior and student achievement," *American Educational Research Journal* 15: 416–432.

Pope, M. L., and Keen, T. R. (1981): *Personal Construct Psychology and Education*, London, Academic Press.

Popham, J. W. (1975): "Validated instructional materials as the focus of effective curriculum strategy," in J. Schaffarzick and D. H. Hampson (eds.), *Strategies for Curriculum Development*, Berkeley, Calif., McCutcheon.

Popkewitz, T. S. (1984): *Paradigm and Ideology in Educational Research*, London, Falmer Press.

Reid, W. (1988): "Where is the habit of deliberation? in N. Sabar, J. Rudduck, and W. Reid (eds.), *Partnership and Autonomy in School-based Curriculum Development*, USDE Papers in Education, University of Sheffield.

Reid, W. A., and Walker, D. F. (eds.) (1975): *Case Studies on Curriculum Change*, London, Routledge and Kegan Paul.

Reynolds, A., Hayrose, J., Ringstuff, C., and Grossman, P. (1988): "Teachers and curriculum materials: Who is driving whom?" *Curriculum Perspectives* 8, 1: 22–29.

Ricoeur, P. (1974): *The Conflict of Interpretations*, Evanston, Ill., Northwestern University Press.

―――― (1981): *Hermeneutics and the Human Sciences*, Cambridge, Cambridge University Press.

Roberts, D. A., and Russell, T. L. (1975): "An alternative approach to science education research: Drawing from philosophical analysis to examine practice," *Curriculum Theory Network* 5, 2: 107–125.

Robinsohn, S. B. (1969): "A conceptual structure of curriculum development," *Comparative Education* 5, 3: 221–234.

Rudduck, D. (1987): "Can school-based curriculum development be other than conservative?" in N. Sabar, J. Rudduck, and W. Reid (eds.), *Partnership and Autonomy in School-based Curriculum Development*, USDE Papers in Education, University of Sheffield.

Rudduck, J. (1988): "The ownership of change as a basis for teachers' professional learning," in J. Calderhead (ed.), *Teachers' Professional Learning*, London, Falmer Press, pp. 205–222.

Russell, T. (1988): "From pre-service teacher education to first year of teaching: A study of theory and practice," in J. Calderhead (ed.), *Teachers' Professional Learning*, London, Falmer Press, pp. 13–34.

Sabar, N., Rudduck, J., and Reid, W. A. (eds.) (1987): *Partnership and Autonomy in School-based Curriculum Development*, USDE Papers in Education, University of Sheffield.

Sarason, S. (1982): *The Culture of School and the Problem of Change*, Boston, Allyn and Bacon, 1st edition 1971.

Schumacher, E. F. (1978): *A Guide for the Perplexed*, London, Cox and Wyman, pp. 9–23.

Schwab, J. J. (1964): "Problems, topics and issues," in S. Elam (ed.), *Education and the Structure of Knowledge*, Chicago, Rand McNally, pp. 4–47.

—————— (1966): "The teaching of science as enquiry," in J. J. Schwab and P. F. Brandwein, *The Teaching of Science*, Cambridge, Mass., Harvard University Press, pp. 1–103.

—————— (1969): "The practical: A language for curriculum," *School Review* 78, 1: 1–23.

—————— (1973): "The practical 3: Translation into curriculum," *School Review* 81: 501–522.

—————— (1983): "The practical 4: Something for curriculum professors to do," *Curriculum Inquiry* 13, 3: 239–265.

Science Teachers' Association of Ontario (1985): "A rationale for quality science education in the schools of Ontario, Toronto," author.

Shipman, M. D., Bolam, D., and Jenkins, D. R. (1974): *Inside a Curriculum Project: A Case Study in the Process of Curriculum Change*, London, Methuen.

Shulman, L. S. (1986): "Those who understand: Knowledge growth in teaching," *Educational Research* 15, 3: 4–14.

Shulman, L. S. (1987): "Knowledge and teaching: Foundations of the new reform," *Harvard Educational Review* 57, 1: 1–22.

Silberstein, M. (1982): "Curriculum development and interpretation as a subject in pre-service training program in Israel," Israeli Curriculum Development Centre, Ministry of Education and Culture, Jerusalem.

Silberstein, M., and Ben-Peretz, M. (1983): "The use of syllabus analysis in teacher education programs," in P. Tamir, A. Hofstein, and M. Ben-Peretz (eds.), *Preservice and Inservice Training of Science Teachers*, Philadelphia, Rehovot, Balaban International Science Services.

———— (1987): "The concept of teacher autonomy in curriculum materials: An operative interpretation," *Journal of Curriculum and Supervision* 3, 1: 29–44.

Skilbeck, M. (1984): *School-based Curriculum Development*, London, Harper and Row.

———— (1987): "School-based curriculum development and central curriculum policies in England and Wales: A paradox in three acts," in N. Sabar, J. Rudduck, and W. Reid (eds.), *Partnership and Autonomy in School-based Curriculum Development*, USDE Papers in Education, University of Sheffield, pp. 16–27.

Stenhouse, L. (1979): "Case study in comparative education: Particularity and generalization," *Comparative Education* 15, 1: 5–10.

———— (ed.) (1980): *Curriculum Research and Development in Action*, London, Heineman.

Tamir, P., and Glassman, F. (1971): "A practical examination for BSCS students: A progress report," *Journal of Research in Science Teaching* 8: 307–315.

Taylor, P. H. (1970): *How Teachers Plan Their Courses*, Slough, England, National Foundation for Educational Research.

Taylor, W. (1978): *Research and Reform in Teacher Education*, Slough, England, National Foundation for Educational Research.

Tilemma, H. H., and De Jong, R. (1986): "Teachers' task perception and professional competencies," paper presented at the

1986 conference of the International Study Association on Teacher Thinking (ISATT), Leuven, Belgium, October 14–17.

Tyler, R. W. (1949): *Basic Principles of Curriculum and Instruction*, Chicago, University of Chicago Press.

Vigotsky, L. S. (1978): *Mind in Society: The Development of Higher Psychological Processes* Essays edited by M. Cole, V. John-Steinger, S. Scribner, and E. Souberman, Cambridge, Mass., Harvard University Press.

Walker, D. F. (1974): "A naturalistic model for curriculum development," *School Review* 79, 1: 51–65.

Westbury, I. (1972): "The character of a curriculum for a 'practical' curriculum," *Curriculum Theory Network* 10: 25–36.

Zahorik, I. A. (1975): "Teachers' planning models," *Educational Leadership* 33: 134–139.

Curriculum Materials

The Animal and Its Environment (1969): Centre for Curriculum Development, Ministry of Education and Culture, Jerusalem, Maalot.

Biological Science: An Inquiry into Life (1971): Jerusalem, Israeli Science Teaching Center.

Bonstingel, J. J. (1985): *Introduction to the Social Sciences*, Teachers' Guide and Resource Book, Boston, Allyn and Bacon.

Creative Role Playing in Science and Technology (CREST) (1986): Social Science Consortium Inc., Boulder, Col.

Department of Education (State of Hawaii) (1977): *Environmental Education in Hawaii*, revised version, Honolulu.

English Alpha Teachers' Edition (1982): K. Sutherland (ed.), Boston, Houghton Mifflin.

Lessons in History (1974): Schavit et al., Tel-Aviv, Maalot.

"Listening," Teachers' Handbook (1977): Centre for Curriculum Development, Ministry of Education and Culture, Jerusalem, and Centre of Curriculum Development, University of Haifa.

"Man and Water," Teachers' Guide (1975): *Man in Nature Series*, Jerusalem, Curriculum Centre, Ministry of Education and Culture.

"Man in Nature—Man and Water," Centre for Curriculum Development, Ministry of Education and Culture, Jerusalem, and Division of Curriculum Planning, School of Education, Haifa University, trial edition (1974): M. Ben-Peretz (ed.), with N. Buras, Z. Dubinski., S. Carmel, and R. Tzernik (commercial edition 1978).

"Man in Nature—Man and Landscape," Centre for Curriculum Development, Ministry of Education and Culture, Jerusalem, and Division of Curriculum Planning, School of Education,

Haifa University, trial edition (1975): M. Ben-Peretz (ed.), with Z. Naveh, N. Buras, Z. Dubinski, S. Carmel, P. Sivan, and R. Tzernik (commercial edition 1980).

"Man in Nature—The Uniqueness of Man: Homo Sapiens," Centre for Curriculum Development, Ministry of Education and Culture, Jerusalem, and Division of Curriculum Planning, School of Education, Haifa University, trial edition (1975): M. Ben-Peretz (ed.), with R. Eshenheimer, E. Hammerstein, L. P. Panso, R. Rosenthal, P. Sivan, and S. Witenhoff (commercial edition 1980).

"Man in Nature—The Uniqueness of Man: The Nervous System—Individualized Version," Centre for Curriculum Planning, School of Education, Haifa University, trial edition (1975): M. Ben-Peretz (ed.), with R. Eshenheimer, E. Hammerstein, L. Panso, R. Rosenthal, P. Sivan, and S. Witenoff (commercial edition 1980).

"People and Resources," Teachers' Guide (1975): London, Evans Brothers.

Schavit, S., et al. (1974): *Lessons in History: The Teachers Handbook*, Tel-Aviv, Maalot.

"The Plant and Its Environment: Plants and Water" (1974): M. Silberstein (ed.), with M. Ben-Peretz, M. Zaharoni, B. Nachman, and A. Sivan, Tel-Aviv, Maalot.

Appendix

CURRICULUM ANALYSIS MATRIX
(BEN-PERETZ 1977, 1978)

The following statements reflect different possible expressions of orientations in curriculum materials. Please rate the degree to which each statement is representative of the materials in the following way:

1 — not at all
2 — somewhat
3 — to a large extent

Dimension No. 1: Subject Matter

	1 Not at all	2 Somewhat	3 To a large extent
Category 1.10. Information, concepts, principles.			
1.11. The materials present specific information.			
1.12. The materials emphasize unifying concepts.			
1.13. The materials emphasize general principles.			
Category 1.20. Approaches to the nature of scientific inquiry.			
1.21. The materials imply the existence of a general mode of inquiry.			
1.22. The materials present specific methodologies for different research problems.			

	1 Not at all	2 Somewhat	3 To a large extent
Category 1.30. Relationship to every- day life.			
1.31. The materials convey the meaning of subject matter knowledge for individuals.			
1.32. The materials express the meaning of subject matter knowledge for society.			
Category 1.40. Image of scientist.			
1.41. Scientists and scholars are mentioned anony- mously.			
1.42. Scientists and scholars are mentioned by name.			
1.43. The personal back- ground of scholars is described.			
Category 1.50. Integration with other disciplines.			
1.51. The materials present knowledge from vari- ous disciplines as a prerequisite for under- standing.			
1.52. The materials present transfer of knowledge from one discipline to another.			

Dimension No. 2: Learner

Category 2.1. Image of learner			
2.11. The learner is involved in active discovery learning.			

	1 Not at all	2 Somewhat	3 To a large extent
2.12. The learner is expected to acquire knowledge that is presented in the textbook.			
Category 2.20. Opportunities for learner development.			
2.21. The materials offer opportunities for cognitive development.			
2.22. The materials offer opportunities for affective involvement.			
2.23. The materials offer opportunities for psychomotor development.			
Category 2.30. Intended focus of instruction			
2.31. The learner is perceived as an individual with particular needs and interests.			
2.32. The learner is perceived as a member of a group with shared interests and needs.			
Category 2.40. Learning style.			
2.41. The learner is perceived as being able to function in a variety of learning environments, structured or unstructured.			
2.42. The learner is perceived as requiring a highly structured learning environment.			

	1 Not at all	2 Somewhat	3 To a large extent

Dimension No. 3: Milieu

Category 3.10. Interaction between society and the discipline.

3.11. Influences of society on the development of the discipline are explicitly mentioned in the materials.

3.12. Influences of the development of the discipline on society are explicitly mentioned in the materials.

Category 3.20. Interaction between society and the process of curriculum development.

3.21. Curriculum materials reflect societal needs.

3.22. Curriculum materials reflect ideological concerns.

Dimension No. 4: Teacher

Category 4.10. Communication of developers' considerations to teachers.

4.11. The teachers' guide relates developers' considerations regarding selection of subject matter.

	1 Not at all	2 Somewhat	3 To a large extent
4.12. The teachers' guide explains the rationale of the developers regarding students.			
4.13. The teachers' guide deals explicitly with developers' considerations regarding the milieu in which the curriculum is to be implemented.			
4.14. The teachers' guide discusses anticipated roles for teachers implementing the materials.			
Category 4.20. Degree of teacher autonomy.			
4.21. Specific objectives are stated.			
4.22. Teaching strategies are specified.			
4.23. Background materials are included in the curriculum package.			
4.24. Teachers are offered teaching alternatives.			
4.25. Teachers are advised to develop their own units.			
Category 4.30. Teachers' role in instruction.			
4.31. The materials suggest a central role for teachers as sources of subject matter knowledge.			

	1 Not at all	2 Somewhat	3 To a large extent
4.32. The materials suggest a supportive role for teachers who guide their students in independent learning.			
Category 4.40. Consideration of teachers' needs			
4.41. Developers manifest awareness of the need for special training in order to teach the program.			
4.42. Possible difficulties in teaching the materials are anticipated.			
4.43. The teachers' guide deals with interpersonal relationships (teacher-student; teacher-parent etc.).			
4.44. The teachers' guide reflects consideration of teachers' opinions and attitudes.			

Index